The Toy of the Spirit

The Toy of the Spirit

Anthony Mannix

PUNCHER & WATTMANN

First published in 2019
Published by Puncher and Wattmann
PO Box 279
Waratah NSW 2298

http://www.puncherandwattmann.com

A catalogue record for this book is available from the National Library of Australia

ISBN 9781925780284

Cover design by Anthony Mannix

Designed and Typeset in Baskerville BT 12/24/48 pt by Gareth Jenkins

Printed by Lightning Source International

The Toy of the Spirit

Anthony Mannix

All Narratives of the
Truth are Psychotic.

Contents

Art of Being
Being of Art

Dr Gareth Jenkins

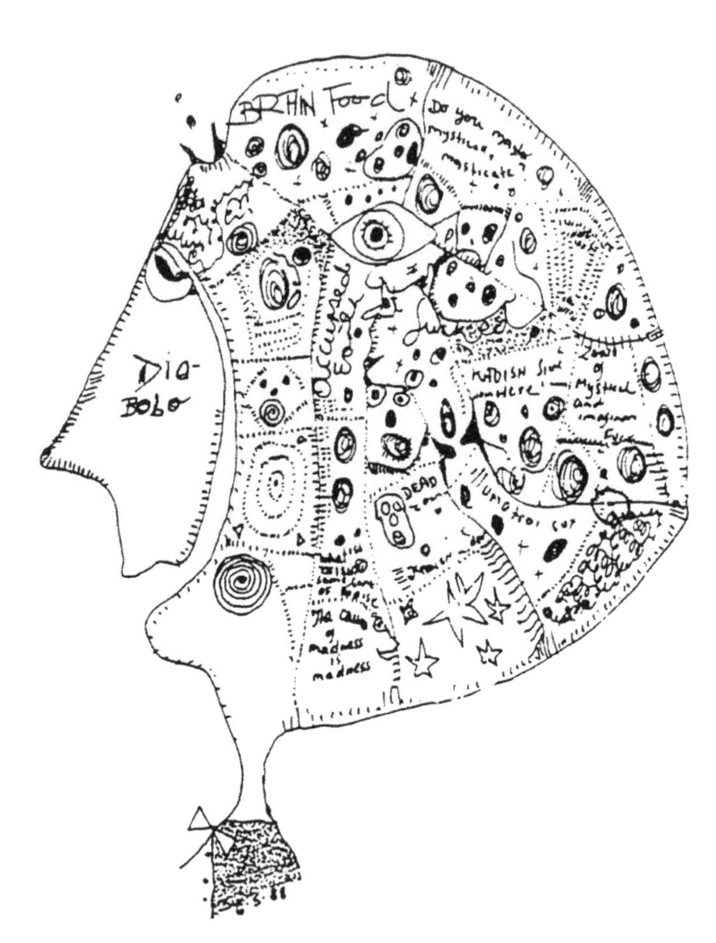
BRAIN Food
Dia-
Bobo
DEAD
madness
is
madness

How to introduce Anthony Mannix?

A list perhaps?

He does like lists:

Anthropologist of the unconscious

Artist Displaced shaman Homeless guy

Maker of schizophrenic sculptures

Writer Locked up lunatic
The Man Who Smokes

Playboy of the garbage tin Friend

Madman Collaborator

Anatomical bomb maker

Cosmologist.

All these people are dead!

I'm going to introduce Mannix to you the way he was introduced to me and the way I have introduced him to others over the last 12 years when I tell them about the work we have been doing together. Together, because I have always worked collaboratively with Mannix; none of my research about his work could have been done in any other way.

In 2005 I was giving a paper at UTS on three authors who I thought I was writing my PhD about: Francis Webb, Unica Zürn and Antonin Artaud – all writers who had experienced aspects of what is currently called schizophrenia. After my talk I hear a voice yell out:

> 'All these people are dead! Are you doing anyone who is alive?'
> 'I don't know any,' I said 'but I'd like to.'
> 'Right then, I know this guy in the Blue Mountains – I'll take you there – if he likes you he might show you some of his books.'

This person in the audience turns out to be the poet Philip Hammial, Mannix's long-time friend and co-founder (with Mannix) of The Australian Collection of Outsider Art.

A few weeks later I find myself wading through an overgrown vacant lot towards Mannix's home in Blackheath, Phil waving me on.

Mannix's house now, as it was then, is a ramshackle assemblage of rooms that look like they are held together by the art that is piled everywhere – walls, floors and all exposed surfaces. He sits in a big armchair facing the French doors through which you enter – he is smoking – he is always smoking. If you visit him now you'll see beside the chair a huge mound of cigarette butts. Underneath the mound is the contract he and I signed back in 2006 setting out the rights and responsibilities of each of us as we embarked on the work of documenting his books – we've never had cause to refer to it again. Last week we joked about my daughter's nickname for him: The Man Who Smokes – he likes that. For her, he will always be that silhouetted hulk of a man on the darkened grounds of the Orange Regional Gallery, the contours of his face sporadically illuminated by the glow of his cigarette.

When I arrive on that first day with Phil there are some books already out but it is only after a long conversation about Artaud, R.D. Laing, Jung, Art Brut and Surrealism that they are opened. I instantly know that I want to include this work in my research. That afternoon we go across the road to the newsagency to photocopy some of the pages so I can read them more closely. In the coming days I realise my entire project needs to be about the work of Anthony Mannix. And that's what it becomes.

What I ultimately found in those books was a rich collection of drawings, paintings and writings in ink, tea, varnish, graphite, wax, pen, dirt, charcoal, texta – Mannix has utilised anything that can make a mark over his many years of compulsive creation. His texts range widely in approach, employing humour and poetry, diaristic reflection, creative writing, heart-felt emotion, anthropological cataloguing, description and explanation. Text is often skilfully integrated with imagery to at once narrate and embellish: at times written with calligraphic design, or dashed-off functionality; at others typed with a typewriter or ink-stamped around images characterised by bold colouration, assured figurative illustration and abstracted design.

As far as subject matter is concerned, Mannix's work centres on the documentation and investigation of his experiences of 'madness' and, what is for him, madness' implicit creativity. By turns visionary, philosophical and erotic, Mannix's creative practice, in all its varied manifestations, is an anthropological engagement with his journeys through unconscious worlds.

> It is interesting to consider the hallucination. It comes from the unconscious world and has truth buried in the language of that world. It has an emotional, almost occult impact and everything is seen in an instant. This is the meaning of a great deal of my art – to be the documenter and to some degree a translator of these strange occurrences. [1]

Mannix's career as an art maker now spans over 40 years and has come to include writings, drawings, paintings, sculptures, artists' books and sound recordings. His work is held in numerous private and public collections around Australia and internationally, including the National Gallery of Australia, National Library of Australia, NSW State Library, Wollongong Art Gallery, Wollongong University, Orange Regional Gallery, and the State Library of Queensland. A recent acquisition by The Museum of Everything in London lead to his inclusion in a major exhibition at Tasmania's Museum of Old and New Art (MONA) in 2017/18.

Mannix has regularly exhibited his pictorial work but rarely have his writings been read or published. Until now they have been predominantly contained in approximately 100 one-off, hand written or typewriter written artists books and manuscripts that number roughly 7000 pages.

Whilst his hallucinatory subject matter draws Mannix's work towards the fantastic, his book making practice has always grounded it in the language of everyday materials; a language which encompasses the weight and texture of sharp glass shards; of violently perforated copper plates; of copper wire; of waxed twine; of glass button inlays adorned with the golden head of an ancient Greek soldier; of varnished muslin; of hand-made paper, rice paper, cartridge paper, butcher's paper, blotting paper, sand-paper, card board, plastic and Perspex; that speaks through the weight of a solid timber box with delicately cast feet and the squeal of metallic hinges as an unwieldy wooden front cover is opened; a language of fragility, where each turn of a page imbues the viewer with the fear that the work itself will disintegrate.

Mannix's is a language of the hand-worked object: books stitched with cotton, with copper, builder's thread and industrial twine through holes bored, drilled and punched. Found books are appropriated and transformed: Guard Books, photo albums, company and accounting ledgers, diaries, small notebooks covered in blue plastic or bound in red and black paper; Universal notebooks, and entire published works embellished and transformed. A book of Braille which came to tell two stories: a submerged text signified by the physical landscape of Braille under the fingers and the textual and pictorial work which Mannix created over it.

Shortly after meeting Mannix I began the process of documenting these artist books: 'How many are there?' I ask: 'I don't know,' he replies, 'I just do them and put them in The Room.' He points to a room I have never entered. 'Maybe there's 30?'

After a year of digitally documenting every page of every book he showed me I thought we must be getting close to the end. Then he says: 'There are a few more yet'. In the end I documented 72 books totaling some 5000 pages. These books are stored as PDF files in the digital archive I created with my father to house the work and is called The Atomic Book[2] – the name highlighting the interconnected nature of all Mannix's creative endeavours:

> Every project i initiate emigrates thru the entire substance of my work. To date this 'book of life' is about fifty volumes strong … i spoke to Phillip Hammial during 1984 … i told him i wished to make an "atomic book" … perhaps i meant anatomical bomb. [Ellipsis in original][3]

This idea of a totality of sense making is central to Mannix's creative practice, where all works contribute to the development of a vast interconnected cosmology articulating his experience of worlds within worlds. To this effect he's called his oeuvre an anthropology of the unconscious, the art of schizophrenia, the atomic book, the book of life and a being of art (as opposed to a body of work).

One of the most obvious ways this interconnectivity manifests itself in Mannix's work is the melding of his two primary creative impulses – text and image. Whilst the focus of this publication is on Mannix's most text-driven material, images have been included to complement the writing, as was the case in the original artist books from which all the texts are drawn. Mannix describes the process of creating integrated works of the pictorial and the textual as akin to welding with a powerful and precise machine: 'The marvel i think one never accepts is that immense constant Potency whereby with nothing more than a pen one can weld together picture and word as if one is using precise and powerful means of machinery.

That inchoate point is the end of the welding tip where everything is flux.'[4]

Created over a long period of time in all manner of places and states of mind these artist books are Mannix's most guarded possessions – a 'very great treasure' he calls them. 'There are books I'll never part with,' he says, 'because they're from precious times and because of the cleanliness with which they actually look at those mechanisms of creation that made them. I understand those books – they are very familiar and yet very alien, but very comforting.'

In the work selected for *The Toy of the Spirit*, the reader gains a glimpse into Mannix's 'mechanisms of creation'. The texts are presented chronologically in the order in which they were written and constitute the first and only publication of the selected writings of Anthony Mannix. All were initially written between 1985 and 1994 – what Mannix calls his 'writing period'. But writing, in its many forms has always held an important place in Mannix's creative practice over the last 40 years:

> The thing that makes me write only occurs every two or three or four years. It's a mechanical review of the things in my life. They get the language of the times and my work, and help me to understand the changes, to pose problems and also to resolve and sum everything up. A piece of writing might be done after several years of activity have come to a conclusion. And it's a neat little parcel now. So, then you can actually look at it and write about it.[5]

Like all of Mannix's creative practice, writing is functional, helping to document, to resolve issues, to reflect on his experiences. To collect and publish these writings has given Mannix fresh opportunities to understand change, to interrogate problems and come to conclusions. This publication is both the continuation of Mannix's obsession with self-reflexive book making and another venture all together – a step away from the hand written, one-off creations steeped in intense materiality towards a form of mass production. How well do these pages, unmarked by the maker's finger prints and hand-written script, maintain the treasured state of the original? How well do they capture the precious times in which they were written? How familiar or alien or comforting will the reader find them?

The Aberrant Paths

> i might have been destined for an illustrious career in writing surrealism had i not gone mad and avoided them and gone mad in such manner as to lead to outsider writing and the aberrant paths … [Ellipsis in original][6]

How to contextualise Mannix's written work? He is, of course, already out there in front of me calling it Outsider Writing in a self-reflexive manoeuvre that at once destabilises the definition. He's done this with his visual art too and it is this very self-awareness that troubles the term 'Outsider'. But this term has always been troubled. From the foundational notion that the work of quintessential figures like Adolf Wölfli came from a deep inner place of pure creativity without reference to the wider world; to the lack of understanding of the influence these so called Outsiders have often exerted on the Insider art mainstream (see the relationship between Prinzhorn's *Artistry of the Mentally Ill* and the Surrealist group as one example); to the more recent curatorial moves to erode the distinction between Outsider and Insider in favour of a more fluid view of what constitutes art in mainstream exhibitions: the 2013 Venice Biennale is a high profile example of this, with organisations such as MONA and The Museum of Everything also playing a significant global role in de-ghettoising, so called Outsider Art – bringing it to a wider audience by sidestepping the term all together; instead it becomes charismatic art displayed with the level of care it deserves.

Where does that leave Mannix, self-appointed Outsider Artist and Writer? Well interestingly it seems to maintain his status as Other to the mainstream, leaving him right where he has always been, in the margins – a zone of instability that defies external, fixed definitions. He is that intriguing and unique combination of a writer driven to create by powerful impulses, often outside his conscious control, and an anthropologist of his own creations, building new systems for understanding his world-view which sees psychotic experiences as meaningful and valuable and powerfully illuminating.

Other writers that give his work context include builders of great textual cosmologies driven by madness – Outsiders like Adolf Wölfli and Henry Darger; anthropologists of their own madness like Emanuel Swedenborg and Daniel Schreber; fringe literary figures like Unica Zürn who used their experiences of madness as inspiration for autobiographical and creative works and finally Antonin Artaud.

Artaud is perhaps the best fit; a writer who has been a direct inspiration to Mannix and one who, like Mannix, wrote from within psychosis (*Artaud the Momo*) and created searing social commentary about the situation and plight of the mad (*Van Gogh, the Man Suicided by Society*).

Words I hear around me are deadly potent

So what does Mannix actually mean when he calls his work Outsider Writing?

Allen S. Weiss sums up his position well, going back to the seminal figure Jean Dubuffet who coined the term Art Brut (anglicised later as Outsider Art by Roger Cardinal in his book of the same name):

> Jean Dubuffet – who in 1945 began his research into Art Brut, those rare, radically inventive or bizarre artistic works of people situated at the margins of culture: the mad, the isolated, the eccentric – established the parallel notion of écrits bruts to account for those texts which do not fall under our standard cultural purview. Here, the standard genres and narrative forms of literary and discursive writing are overturned: vocabulary is reinvented, syntax shattered, and orthography transformed.[7]

Language, that shared system for understanding, is uniquely suited to highlighting this overturning of fixed definitions and this is a hallmark of Outsider Writing, of which Antonin Artaud is archetypal. The work of Outsider Writers exceeds even the limits of literature itself, charting the outer edges of rational or discursive language use defined by Jed Rasula and Steve McCaffery as 'the exploration and exercise of tolerable linguistic deviance.' Thus, they suggest: 'the institutional custodianship of literature serves mainly to protect the literary work from language, shielding it from the disruptive force of linguistic slippage'.[8]

Outsider writing then, perforates the membrane of this 'tolerable linguistic deviance', exposing the full force of the 'linguistic slippage' which rational language use is forever resisting. Such a slippage is built into language systems that can be characterised as a web of arbitrary relations (see Saussure)[9] , a web in which many Outsiders find themselves enmeshed. Their linguistic explorations are less an exercise in experimentation (in a Modernist Steinian / Joycean context) and more an attempt to express or quell their lived experience of language as a powerful and often unstable instrument for interacting with their animate world.

'Plurality and the Ollu-din' for example, is no experiment. Completed while homeless under a street light next to the Art Gallery of NSW it is Mannix grappling with paradox and ambiguity – concepts he returns to time and time again in his writing as the deep unstable heart of his psychotic experience of reality.

> Plurality and the Ollu-din
>
> consequentially, with reference,
> and reference to, it is considered,
> [and to be considered], that in due
> course and to some finalization, to
> an extent and to a degree the
> differences and differences that will
> lead to alliance do not substantially
> outweigh those of the same, as
> mentioned above, respectively, which,
> will not lead to alliance … [10]

For the Outsider Writer, language itself is at times defamiliarised (in Shklovsky's use of the word)[11] and reconfigured in order to depict experiences which conventional rational language use is incapable of capturing.

Here, shared grammatical and denotative rules breakdown and conventional meaning is distorted as language is bent to communicate with Mannix's hallucinatory 'presences' or reinvented to approach the internal lived experience of psychosis. For Mannix, language becomes a tool for interacting with psychotic experiences but is also a weapon that can be used against him by the 'forces' present during psychosis:

> The words I hear around me are deadly potent. If I could wield the thought like solid matter how much would I destroy and how much would I make? I want to see the madnesses expounded, for how else are these unborn children that one sees in the plethora of beings to be laid to earth quietly, quickly and with appropriate ceremony?[12]

As is depicted here, the concretisation of imagined worlds through hallucination or psychosis has been described as a 'lived metaphor'.[13] For Mannix, the imaginative or metaphoric constructs he thinks and writes about can come to constitute his reality concretely; in this way, for Mannix, language recovers its ritual, occult associations, wherein the Word has capacity to literally transform his bodily reality.

> Every thought I think impales me through the vital organs. Through every tender thing that I possess. It is as if becoming clearer this exile. It seems. And in seeming it becomes. I can not venture forth in my imagination for fear that it will become the real article that it will become solid matter. The imagination I am dealing with is that horrendous, that apocalyptic, that bizarre. Such a small thing as beauty will take me into the realms of demons of animalism, to the great waterfalls of the neurotic speculation, to the great iron floor of psychosis. I think therefore I am. And in being let loose uncontrollable wild screams.[14]

The 'uncontrollable wild screams' of Mannix's individualistic voice are everywhere evident in his work, work unashamedly driven by his madness and its eroticism. Mannix admits the instability of madness into language so as to more fully communicate his experience of psychosis, raising his voice against the silencing impulses of the mental institutions and their medical models that he has been incarcerated in time and time again over the last 40 years. Christof Migone articulates the impact of these drivers on the language use by Outsiders:

> The Brut's writings are authored by people who spent the better part of their lives in institutions … The texts are embodied, because we have straightjacketed them. These texts are bodies. They scream, masturbate, contort, fuck, defecate, digest, exercise, cough, sweat, etc. They are not necessarily or exclusively loud or scatological, but they are undeniably tied to the individual rather than untied or strapped to the body of the institution of literature.[15]

Mannix's texts are certainly 'bodies' – they do masturbate, fuck and sweat. He writes:

> 'I feel I am embedded in some great sexual organ that needs a spark to ignite it'[16]
>
> He writes:
>
> 'I am fresh from a dream and it has left my body stinging with the tincture of burning sulphur, with the scent of carbolic acid, with the stench of faeces and of rotten meat'[17]
>
> He writes:

> 'Through a lascivious gorge narcotic zephyrs came giving me visions of immense, outlandish, disobedient flowers and sense of bareness I had never known. I did dark dances about the nipples until everything became odorous and sweaty and great stupa loomed in the air like those of the Borobudur.'[18]

This last quote is from the opening pages of "The Light Bulb Eaters". It is handwritten in Mannix's distinctive script in a number of different pens, arrows show where additions to the text have been added and the paper smells like tobacco.

Is the text more embodied in its original form?
More Outsider?
I'd have to say yes.

It's undeniable that the process of selecting, typing up and editing that Mannix and I have undertaken to prepare these texts for publication, and their very publication in a mass produced book have, inevitably, brought them closer to literature's Inside. Nonetheless, they retain the 'tincture of burning sulphur', the outlandish visions, the radicalised grammar, the looming stupas, the neologisms, the 'great sexual organs' often captured in chaotic, loosely associative or what I have called 'speculative narratives' which ensure they remain resolutely tied to Mannix and his project of anthropological self investigation and definition.

Interestingly, as obscure as Mannix's work can be at times he would say he always strives for clarity, for communication, it's just that some of the experiences are so 'irreal' that to present them accurately from his perspective results in material that no longer uses language in its conventional denotative sense. Here I'm talking about works which exist on a continuum between language and image: sex-scribble[19], the wheeled ideas[20], and glossolalia.[21] These works are currently available only in Mannix's artist books and their digital representation in the Atomic Book Archive; they await the intrepid explorer. The works in this current collection then, can be seen as a point of entry; the undulating surface of Mannix's deep Outsider practice.

Riding the Beast sidesaddle

So, even if this publication process has brought the included work further Inside, Mannix's close involvement in the selection and editing process ensures that this shift has been on his own terms and that he continues to speak with his own voice. My own editing influence has been purposefully light in order to ensure that Mannix maintains control of his own narrative, which has always been a primary concern for an individual who has spent so many years resisting the monologue of psychiatry hell-bent on re-writing him and his experiences so that it adheres to the structures of the medical model. It was no good of course; Mannix always managed to subvert psychiatry's 'process' as he calls it:

> I find the exact same circumstances occurring to me again & again. There is a night of 'drama' which is the culmination of months of madness. It is usually a very 'fast' night, the Police are there and usually the ambulancemen. My heart and soul sink as i am driven by them to the asylum. In the passing scenery i see the destruction of all the aspirations i held and the things i painstakingly built. I am "admitted". I have a terrible night. In the morning the 'Process' begins. Usually two or so weeks later, the Gods that be, who comprehend everything but understand nothing take my repeated pleas into account, and these Public Hospital Doctors 'allow' me again possession of my clothing. Whereupon i make my way to the local Newsagent, buy some very cheap paper and an artline pen. After i 'hide' anywhere

> on the Asylum grounds away from troublesome aspects (people) and draw.[22]

Creative self expression becomes not only a coping mechanism for the boredom and regimented depersonalisation of the institution, but it is through art making that Mannix both preserves his 'personal history' and begins again to re/create the world which 'reality' has destroyed. He writes specifically of this: 'after two or three weeks of extreme agitation in a hospital, I would go out and draw – as if to piece things together again; as if not to lose the manner of seeing that existed'.[23]

Language too is a powerful tool in this endeavour, well read in psychiatry and psychology, Mannix regularly radicalises their terminology by showing these labels to be, merely, clinical terms for what he experiences as palpable, animated presences.

> i am burning the last of my childhood photographs in neurotic annihilation, and the ashes remind me of the feelers of insects. Each night i am confronted with diaphaneous beings, personalities, possessivenesses. Phobia comes one night, Dementia another and Apoplexia and Mania the next and whisper their scream/stare/whisper into me. Its a trance of the low elongated keys, almost beyond the range of human perception, calling again and again. to call it moaning is to ride the Beast sidesaddle.[24]

The beast mentioned here is the unconscious – at times a realm and at times an entity: to ride it 'sidesaddle' is to feminise it or be feminised by it.

Dissertation or Distraction.

> Now, I am writing a dissertation about madness. One (1) it is a state that however much knowledge there is it is never explained. It is a Flux, about which hovers the soul and creative ardour of the 'knower'... Out of madness is born a creative seed which can be used in many, many ways...One must make, really make; ... What madness supplies in the creative process is manifold, not least of all a great and uncomfortable projection in Realms where there are energies that cannot be denied.[25]

This notion of 'Flux' aligns with Mannix's writings on the ideas of Chaos and Paradox he suggests are central to psychotic experience and the unconscious landscapes that hold the unlimited generative opportunities of the 'irreal' freed of denotive restriction:

> To cease to have definition in some way is the access to traversing the unconscious as journey. To pursue this to its root, one must cease the substance of the concept. Then the Myriads do not oppose you.
>
> When the architecture of concept is dissolved one is hit by the storm. This is chaos. No logical argument will deliver you from this place and yet no logic can oppose successfully what you wish to build. Chaos is the climatic and elemental.
>
> Where reality is not subject to vague or bloody connotation one finds the irreal. Its escape from colonization or denotation means that it is mobile, and powerful.[26]

It is this irreal 'manner of seeing' that Mannix documents in all the texts included in this collection. Here he takes us into his unconscious landscapes
where machines are animated and anticipating the doom of their masters
the ageless horse of Psychosis gallops

the Thin Ball-Bearing Man rises up and walks,
Rosey Spite is smoking her cigars after drinks with Castro
and

'The Moon was in The Head but this was wrong because the bone was too dirty, but it was like the moon born dead and rotting and erotic but this was wrong because The Moon was big & open & moist in The Sky … it was like The Head was made from a shit of the moon.'[27]

Spitting wheel of knowledge

Let's take a closer look at the work we selected to include in this book. "Dedications": a list of many of the hallucinatory presences Mannix has encountered in his life. "The Machines, or a Concise History of the Machine (as far as I know them …) …": a series of hand drawn illustrations with accompanying short texts describing otherworldly animate machines. "The Skull": a deep exploration of the minutia of psychotic thought and experience. "The Demise": an apocalyptic narrative where the human race's only hope to maintain connection with the divine is through the mad. "The Light Bulb Eaters", which Mannix describes as his novel, which details what he called the schizophrenic trek and lastly "The People's Odyssey", a series of reflections on outsider artists that he has known.

Dedications

Mannix's work is often a dialogue between himself and the hallucinatory Other, which he calls 'apparitions', 'presences', or 'appearances'.

> My artistic output over the last twenty-five years has had one point and that has been to document the landscape of psychosis and the unconscious. It involves an intuitive invention of cultural anthropology to make some order of the plethora of hallucinations, visions, spirits, ghosts, apparitions, and creatures, which populate this, altered perspective. I have learnt my trade myself; patterns, designs and artefacts I have observed in all worlds go to form a network of technique.[28]

When I first began to document Mannix's work he would carry on conversations with these apparitions in the next room, convincing them that I was not a threat, that I was 'not trying to rip him off'. 'He's alright,' he'd say – 'we can trust him.' Mannix always believed in me it seems, but it was clear the presences were not so sure.

Rather than attempting to exclude these apparitions from his sphere of consciousness, Mannix uses creativity as a tool to interact and manage a psychic environment crowded with personalities, ghosts, demons and doppelgangers. Whilst they certainly pose threats and can be dangerous, many are also his friends, lovers and collaborators.

The most comprehensive inventory of the apparitions Mannix has encountered over his years of psychotic hallucinations are in this list-based work "Dedications". Each dedication is given equal status and this suggests that, as with so many of Mannix's constructions, there is no one fixed hierarchy relating to such entities.

Mannix seems to possess a relationship with each being, and his descriptions often recall the erotic experiences he has had with them; this can be seen in the following example: 'for the re-incarnated Salome who danced with me at night in the empty city amphitheatre … later i found my pants wet, my wallet gone and my throat cut … ' [Ellipsis in original][29]

The list opens, and returns numerous times to some of Mannix's core concerns, the plight of the insane, their disjunction with mainstream society and their ongoing conflict with the medical profession:

> for 'Them', at five o'clock they filtered casually back to their homes and flats and houses in the twilight of summer to drink their drinks and think their thoughts … For 'Us', at five the doors were locked behind us and fourteen hours would pass before being revomited out of the bloody whale … [30]

This list-making is a feature of Mannix's work, and demonstrates the inventive nature of his animated cosmology, specifying the vast range of entities in Mannix's metaphorical realm. As ever this is Mannix as anthropologist documenting what he has experienced and ruminating on the nature of the human experience.

> for The Hidden Self which has the faculty of luminous creativity and conveys messages not only for the individual but for the future of our species … [31]

The Machines, or a Concise History of the Machine (as far as I know them …) …

"The Machines, or a Concise History of the Machine (as far as I know them …) …" is an example of Mannix's ability to meld text and image – a feature of his work throughout his artists books.

Mannix details the inspiration for this series of textual drawings where he writes:

> in the winter of 1985, Philip Hammial came to my flat at Crown St and asked if i would illustrate his book of Poetry. I agreed and drew more than a score of illustrations in a week. They were strange Vehicular entities to match his vehicle poems. The book was of course entitled, "Vehicles"[32]: after which the strange, little animated Vehicle became a permanent recurrence in my drawing. I in turn, one very psychotic night and morning wrote: 'The Concise History of the Machine'. a score or more of little poems relating to the Machine which were recorded by Graeme Revell for a section of a European distributed record.[33]

The machine works that appear in this book have been collected from a number of sources: nine of the works appear in *Journal of a Madman No.5* and two other works were found in a large box of miscellaneous writings.

As Mannix suggests, these works form the basis for a collaboration with the composer Graeme Revell. Entitled "A Concise History of the Machine", it features Mannix reading these works with a musical score by Revell. Here Mannix reads fifteen individual 'Machine' pieces – thus the recording is the most complete record of the original textual creations.[34]

The handwritten script is embellished to highlight the design potential of letters as shapes. The language is compressed and each work is self-contained, in the mode of a poem or prose-poem (he calls them 'little poems'). Each text is written around the accompanying drawing and regularly the drawing and the text intersect; these facts and the decorative nature of the script serve to present a unified field in which the pictorial and the textual are inseparable from one another.

The Skull / a story

"The Skull" tells a short story in paragraph-length vignettes; it possesses a dense ambiguity and a submerged privacy of meaning. This work documents a psychotic experience with a sense of immediacy that draws the reader inside the metaphoric shifting reality of the narrator.

The Skull, in its original form, is a limited edition artist's book created in a run of fifty. Each is printed on a fine textured paper and embellished with original cover artwork.

This narrative was originally created during psychosis, the final printed page in the original books read: 'This Worke 'occurred' during deep psychosis in 1981 ... & was transcribed into manuscript during the summer 1985-86' [Ellipsis in original].[35]

The narrative was then 'transcribed' into the manuscript. This is a concrete rendering of psychotic thought; an attempt to directly present a psychotic experience in language, with all its paradoxes and impossibilities intact.

To this end "The Skull" is an unstable narrative which frequently dissolves into paradoxical impossibility: points where definitive denotation breaks down and meaning spreads into multiple connotations and the confluence of ambiguity.

Here a dialogue between madness and reason is played out in language itself as a tension between rational non-sense and sense. It is at the points of radical associative confluence within the text that true communication occurs. Mannix stresses the importance of such ideas through his inclusion of a quotation from Marcus Aurelius that he uses to open the text.

Cease not to think of the Universe as one living Being, possessed of a single Substance and a single Soul; and how all things trace back to its single sentience; and how it does all things by a single impulse; and how all existing things are joint causes of all things that come into existence; and how intertwined in the fabric is the thread and how closely woven the web.[36]

Denotative thinking (which characterises 'normal' thought patterns), whereby a limited number of ideas are linked at any one time, can be viewed as a unifying gesture. However, in Aurelius' and Mannix's formulation, the limiting of associations in this manner actually prevents the mind from realising that it is all things which are interlinked, not merely a selection of them. The points within Mannix's text at which the conventional sense making function of language break down into paradox become opportunities to experience the limitlessness of the whole.

! For a while The Head was a piece of wood, but it was pretending a masquerade … and then little black moons like trapdoors crept open & these eyes started to growl and stare violently at my feet which on its own world, in its own territory is/are possessed by The Enemy; & these eyes, they ran with a hatred like gigantic waterfalls in a trickle & in Reason which was like an insect made into bone.[37]

Mannix begins his work with an inversion: a head that is pretending to be a piece of wood. Here the reader is presented with the moment after the onset of psychosis. The piece of wood, which is the referent from which Mannix initially creates the lived metaphor of the head, does not actually transform into a head but is, in fact, already the head in disguise – in Mannix's conception he has not constructed a psychotic reality over the physical world but is discovering the reality within the physical.

From the first isolated exclamation mark, "The Skull" is imbued with anxiety and instability. The reader is taken inside Mannix's 'irreal' reality where denotation becomes elastic to the point of disintegration.

The Demise

In "The Demise" Mannix remains cloaked behind the hallucinatory voice of his unnamed narrator as he desperately attempts to resist the automation of Western society so as to maintain his connection with the divine through his 'god': 'The recurrent psychosis, the spitting wheel of knowledge, the burnt out eyes that have destroyed beauty to accomplish knowledge.'[38]

"The Demise", in its original form is the first twenty-one pages of a 50-page unbound series of written works. "The Demise" is one of the texts in which Mannix is most conscious of an audience, with its frequent self-reflexive references to the 'Dear reader' and detailing of the actual mechanisms of its creation – unlike the majority of texts in this collection which were hand written, "The Demise" was written on a typewriter. The narrator writes of physically integrating with the typewriter: 'When I type it seems I am typing in blood. In bloods. I have become like the constructivist machine. I operate. I am efficient. But I betray for I wish to destroy.'[39]

This is a text concerned with words and the power (often mystical) they have to affect the mental and physical reality of the author and reader. It is a text concerned with literary techniques such as metaphor and simile – techniques by which words, at times, ascend to the realm of magic: 'I shake like a leaf and in using this 'simile' become the leaf and must fight.' "The Demise" brings into erratic association the poetic, the narrative and the polemical.

The 'demise' mentioned in the title and referred to within the text itself, does, on one level, relate to the fate of the author. But to a greater degree it is a comment regarding the state of a human race that has lost the capacity to connect with the mystical or divine: 'we are breeding the inhabitants to de-mystify wonders' the narrator tells us at the outset.[40] It is the mad (or those deemed mad) that retain this capacity.

> I am continually calling upon the Gods, and they keep appearing but with different names; different cataclysms and knowing them is like knowing heat in all its wonder – the flames that have poured from me in these 32 years sear the physical material around me. I am careful not to change this reality, at least not too quickly. It will be noted somewhere 'hallucination', 'psychosis', dementia, but still the names choked in the throat. I am perpetual.[41]

Mannix's 'perpetual' narrator tells of the illumination and confusion present in his dialogue with psychosis; tells of itinerant journeys through the city streets and bushlands, of random meetings in art galleries, parties and coffee shops, of the pain of isolation and the wonder of mystical interconnection. This is an apocalyptic text, its landscapes bristling with biblical resonances, ancient gods, doppelgangers, the ghosts of beautiful and disturbing women, and a narrator aware that such experiences can be interpreted as mystical illumination or psychotic delusion.

By the end of "The Demise" the chaos of the narrator's life has been transformed by a purifying psychotic fire – a fire linked to the writing of the text through which the reader becomes a witness to such acts of purification. In Mannix's formulation his kaleidoscopic, speculative narratives born of a dialogue with his 'god' – the 'recurrant psychosis, the spitting wheel of knowledge' – offers the reader insight into the illumination Mannix believes to be present in the 'schizophrenic trek'. A trek Mannix suggests he has most completely described in "The Light Bulb Eaters".

The Light Bulb Eaters

"The Light Bulb Eaters", which Mannix describes as his 'novel', was originally one-hundred and twenty-five hand-written pages bound in an A4-sized artist's sketch book.[42] It is the presentation (at times possessing the spontaneity of a diary) of a sequence of discussions and integrated images in which thoughts, memories and created stories are brought loosely into relation.

Mannix considers "The Light Bulb Eaters" to be the text that most clearly defines his psychotic cosmology. A cosmology possessing an underworld consisting of unconscious 'places' through which he travels on the 'schizophrenic trek'. On such journeys Mannix describes his pursuit of 'power' – a power which allows him to control and create within these places.

He describes the seven psychotic realms of his cosmology, which take the form of concentric circles (the narrative makes specific mention of Dante). Such an organised schema is shown, by Mannix himself however, to be merely a construction, one which cannot remain unified: the chaos and confluence of psychosis render all such borders porous, to the extent that even the supposed centre of this cosmology is unstable and multiple.

It is only in experiencing the unconscious landscape that it can be described or understood. Thus Mannix details his notion of the 'schizophrenic trek' which takes him on challenges through the underworld of the unconscious, an ultimately death-like state. Mannix's own resurrection becomes entwined with his capacity to animate his creative production. His claim, repeated throughout his oeuvre, regarding his experience of art as a living entity is most fully articulated here.

This theme of descent into a deathlike psychotic state and eventual resurrection is the overarching narrative of "The Light Bulb Eaters". It is a journey, Mannix suggests, that 'strikes you dead' – a journey that culminates in the final stages of the text with Mannix shedding his 'body of work' in favour of the animate 'being of art' – at once bringing art and self to life.

The trek itself is effected via art-making (Mannix's 'navigation device' for the psychosis), thus the creation of the text is Mannix's technique for navigating through the unconscious places he describes within it. This is yet another facet of Mannix as anthropologist of the unconscious.

The question remains to be asked, who or what are the light bulb eaters? This phrase, the title of the work, appears on the first page of this book and nowhere else. The illustration that accompanies this title shows a figure sucking from a light bulb that seems to possess a nipple-like teat. This image evokes the notion of an individual sucking at the teat of the unconscious (a formulation that Mannix has elsewhere specifically discussed), emblematic of the opening of a dialogue between rationality and a psychotic unconscious, which the text has attempted to effect.

Mannix however, suggests that the title came from an article he read as a boy in *Reader's Digest*. The article describes the failing attendance at a circus. The sword swallowers employed there attempt to generate interest by swallowing lit light globes mounted on long poles. In this way the innards of the individual were illuminated for the brief amount of time that the performer could keep the bulb in their throat. Thus the light bulb eaters make visible the inside to the outside, a notion that again resonates with Mannix's entire creative project to externally document the unconscious landscapes within him.

The People's Odyssey

"The People's Odyssey" is a series of five poetic prose pieces which focus on different Australian Outsider artists that Mannix knows and admires, many of whom are mentioned in other texts included in this book. Part personal reflection on interactions with the artists, part ekphrasis, they show Mannix's deep engagement with the creative practice and work of others. These works were written and recorded for ABC Radio National on a special entitled 'Outsiders', once again accompanied by the haunting soundscapes of The Loop Orchestra.

The sequence ends with a text on himself – typically self-reflexive:

> 'On Anthony Mannix. "So what?" You may ask. "Here he is. More of his scribbles and his irrational writing."'
>
> Philosophical:
> 'Life has been one step at a time against and ahead of logic, which is not the same as reality.'
>
> Erotic and experimental:
> 'An explosion of the feminine large killzone massive buttocks, prodigious breasts, thighs like tree trunks, all bound up in the captivity of nylon.'[43]

Devouring Definitions

In the creative work included in this collection Mannix creates chaotic, speculative narratives that encompass the fictional, documentary and pictorial. Sitting, just where Mannix likes it, somewhere on the fringes of the Inside and the Outside – that place that resists definitive categorisation:

> An art that is really alive tends to devour its definitions. One realizes very soon that one is given to constructing a beast that will not sit comfortably in the FRAME, and it is the viewer who must adjust to it and not vice versa.[44]

Like the shifting skull that is a head that is a block of wood, this book, the first significant publication of Mannix's writings, provides readers with a series of shifting glimpses of his Being of Art. A being of art that is intent on consuming the reader, reaching outside the FRAME to envelop the viewer in the undulating landscapes Mannix has spent his life exploring and documenting in his role as an anthropologist of the unconscious.

> Writing is a mechanical review of the things in my life,' he says from his armchair, taking a drag of his cigarette. 'It gets the language of the times and my work, and helps me to understand changes, to pose problems and also to resolve and sum everything up. This book publication gives me the concept of legacy now. And of posterity. My words won't end up in the skip bin! I'm not sure what people will make of them. I consider it, again, just part of life in the form of the art of writing. It is of course riddled with imperfections but there was no other way to communicate the intent. People may find it polarizing, I don't know, revolutionary, the conservatives may have a problem with it – but I don't think so.[45]

Polarising, revolutionary or otherwise Anthony Mannix's writing invites the reader on a unique journey and before long you'll feel yourself rubbing shoulders with a host of the pulsating vivid presences and beasts that he has met in his many years of traveling:

Rosey Spite
They
The Obstacle small-radio
the Beast of the Unconscious
Mordrol – bloody dark fish
Christina Farsight
The Black eyes of Destiny
ageless horse of psychosis
Untuck
luminous lighthouse
Milestone
the Lotus
the Little Voice
ghosts of the eternal suicides

The Terror
The Tyger with No Eyes
The thin Ball-Bearing Man
The Giant Pink Fish

Gruesome

Tiberia – the little voice that road
The Doctor
The Eggmen
The Honey-Eater and

The Magnificent Oscillating Vision.

They're all in here

and they are looking forward to meeting you,

come on

come in

the trek is waiting.

Dedications

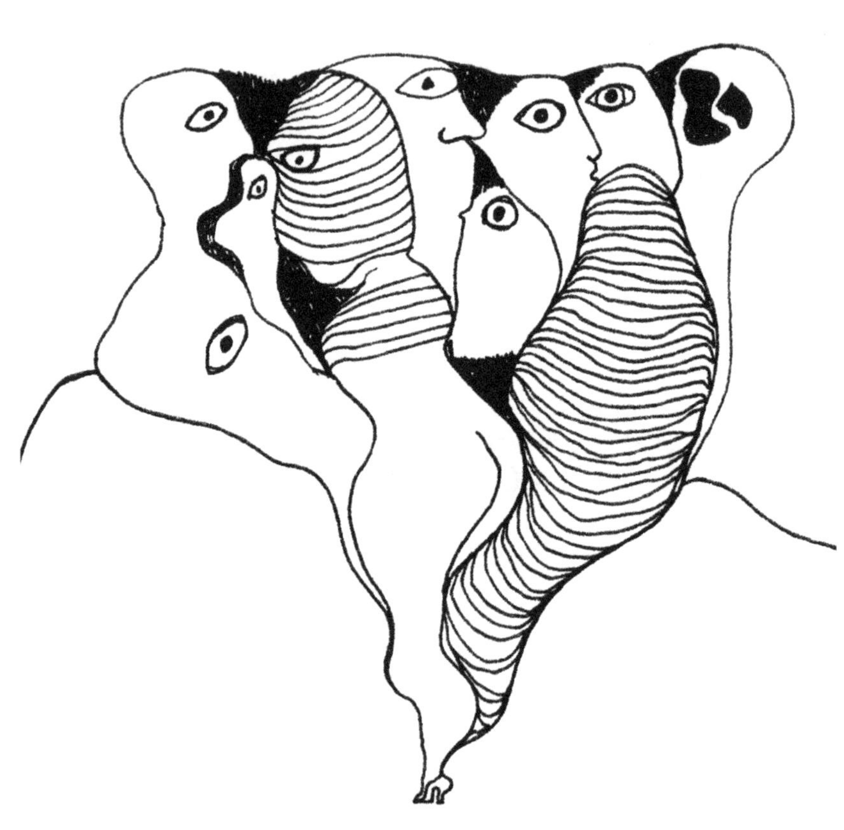

for 'Them', at five o'clock they filtered casually back to their homes and flats and houses in the twilight of summer to drink their drinks and think their thoughts … For 'Us', at five the doors were locked behind us and fourteen hours would pass before being revomited out of the bloody whale …

for The Honey-Bees, sorta nice, sorta nasty desperate strange giant creatures that they were, who seeing the world to live in chose ours, calmly took our form and merged without anyone being the wiser …

for The Vision, whereupon seeing her face, I fell through the trapdoor, landed on the steel spikes and quietly went away, broken and impaled for life …

for The Creel, The Creed, The Crech and their smart-asses associated extra-terrestrial civilizations who invaded. Big deal to their highly developed psychic powers …

for The Ephemeral Nudes who danced in a night molten and aflame with blackness and the men who dissolved into the aether watching them …

for the reincarnated Salome who danced with me at night in the empty city amphitheatre … later I found my pants wet, my wallet gone and my throat cut …

for the old sofa I would work over with a switch-blade knife at night, that summer saw an invigorated release via tantrum never experienced before or since …

for Metamorphose, strange dame, hypnotized me with her lisp, haunted me with her legs, touched me with her curiosity and inflamed me with her viciousness …

for The Moloch which I found creeping around the park alone one night on its ten legs with a zither stuck up its ass, attempting classical music …

for the miasma, the eclipse, the transfiguration and the ecstasy …

for the contradiction, the contrary and the recondite …

for Monotony and vitamin 'B' deficiency which when added in powdered form to the concocting consciousness between the ears leads to weak knees and bubbling Visions of the Perfect …

for the lip complete with moustache, Dylan Thomas writes about finding at night in the Dark straits of Wales … I have been searching for one ever since

for EYE, a monstrous band of suicidal extra-terrestrials with no planet, or orientation and apparently no brains, for not only do they create, explode planets and harness The Overlord, but they are constantly getting trapped in the masterbatoriums and pressing the 'destruct' button instead of the 'start' button in their spaceship …

for Therion, The Overlord, Greasy bastard, I almost managed to cut his balls off when I was only 9 years old …

for Tiberia and her dirty little smile; she led me to a perfect circle which I later found out was circumscribed around myself …

for The Imitations and Their Shadows, strange journey in which I found myself surfacing and blowing out the waters of a nascent and historic sexuality …

for The Tuber-creature which used to dance, sit and exude a silent compassion when I was suffering the devastating physical discomfort of anti-psychotic drugs …

for The Hidden Self which has the faculty of luminous creativity and conveys messages not only for the individual but for the future of our species …

for the ‘typical’ hallucination, the ‘Typical’ delusion and the ‘typical’ derangement …

for the 'garden variety' schizophrenic; may the foliage proliferate …

for the passion of insanity which after being diagnosed, prognosed, unensconced, examined, analysed, labelled, written about and joked upon is calmly and murderously poured down the toilet …

for myself and the other hospital inmates who would regularly, without fail, appear at the ‘Paradise cafe’ every Tuesday night on hospital grounds … sad, vicious irony that it was, it promised a hard sharp little pleasure which worked its way under the skin …

for the words that were never articulated in all the Medication-Rooms as the needles were force-fed into the ass …

for The Shadow, relentless Inspirer … and mild horror … for Dementia, Schizophrenia and Psychosis …

for Kirstina Fatbitch, Christina farsight and Cricket Flybitch, Visions and harmonious Angels …

for Untuck, Entity and the ageless horse of Psychosis, indefatigable, ever-aspected and Mystery …

for Wantid, Entity and the Luminous Lighthouse, awesome, dredged from the Unseen and Milestone …

for Organisation and Method, Orientation and Mobility …

for the words, 'Madman', 'lunatic', 'Derangee' and 'Insane,' and their substance and their salvation from the anaemic labels 'sick' and 'ill' and such petty descriptions as 'off the air' and 'over the tracks' and 'around the bend' …

for Quick Ways, Instant Solutions and lack-of-Means …

for the endless pavement, the endless night, the endless trek and the Endless Vision which indescribably but with great deftness leads to the end of the Tyranny of the Self …

for The Art of Murder and the quivering Phoenix that it holds in its mouth when turned on the self …

for the Art of Demonics, which from its babble and its scorching seeds planted in the sacrum spurt the pollen, the Narcotic …

For Residential, Fascinator, Sensity and Mystere, Women that have occurred, becoming all-encompassing and then dissolved …

for The Ailment, and the dismal science of Speculation which is the Cure …

for The Formula, which down its ever winding, ever-proliferating dark streets and devious alleyways one can become irretrievably lost to one self …

for The Panic, which taken unawares in the New World found itself drowning in a pool of quicksand in the middle of the black streets and its Pleas for Salvation falling on deaf ears …

for The Terror, Alien which it is, once entrenched on the Terra Firma of the abdomen it knows no bounds …

for The Little Voice, which was like the idyll, like a fresh delicate stream …

for Phobia, Mania, Hysteria, Nymphomania and Necromantia, who, jokers that they are, these ghosts of the Eternal Suicides, put me in such a terror when they haunted me with their comrades that I dived head-first through a plate-glass window and woke to find myself floundering in the midst of my own forgotten childhood …

for The Apparition of the Whore which began to appear in my merciless rooms. Alas, I have become jaded to ghosts and did nothing but laugh and try to kiss her …

for Humourie, Sensatione, Macabre and The Cock-Sucker, these women did nothing but try my patience when I was alive, and still continue to do so now that I am dead …

for Hatim, master Javanese whore who in the dark recesses of her eyes I first beheld the music of Debussy, and who informed me that I was to go mad …

for The Eggmen who sent the wonderful resonant percussion music of their planet to me and who for a good portion of a mania infected my life which their pathos and their humour …

for mordrol, bloody dark fish, who when I was desperately seeking a title for a written work sent me to a Kings Cross john where I found a desperado masturbating … 'Genitalia'; being the outcome …

for The Tyger with No Eyes, The Thin Ball-Bearing Man, The Luminous Ghostly Temple, The Giant Pink Fish, Gruesome, The Doctor, the Warlord, The Honey-Eater, The Great Ape and The Magnificent Oscillating Vision, all who at various times I have found indispensable …

The Machines, or a Concise History of the Machine (as far as I know them ...) ...

.O.

1.a

. . . . THE MACHINE APPEARS & disappears WITH RELISH AND ONE is LIABLE to FIND ONESELF ENCUMBERED WITH IT AT THE MOST INAPPROPRIATE AND INOPPORTUNE OF TIMES; OR alternatively, grow SO FOND OF IT THAT IT'S disappearance COMES as a Catastrophic blow...

1.

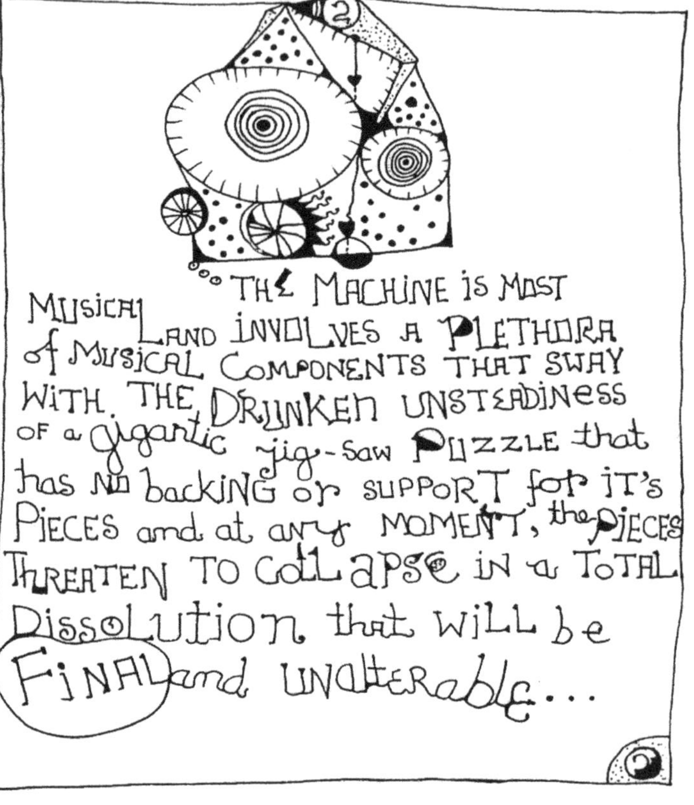
THE MACHINE IS MOST MUSICAL AND INVOLVES A PLETHORA of MUSICAL COMPONENTS THAT SWAY WITH THE DRUNKEN UNSTEADINESS OF a gigantic jig-saw PUZZLE that has NO backING or SUPPORT for IT'S PIECES and at any MOMENT, the PIECES THREATEN TO COLLAPSE IN a TOTAL DISSOLUTION that WILL be FINAL and UNALTERABLE...

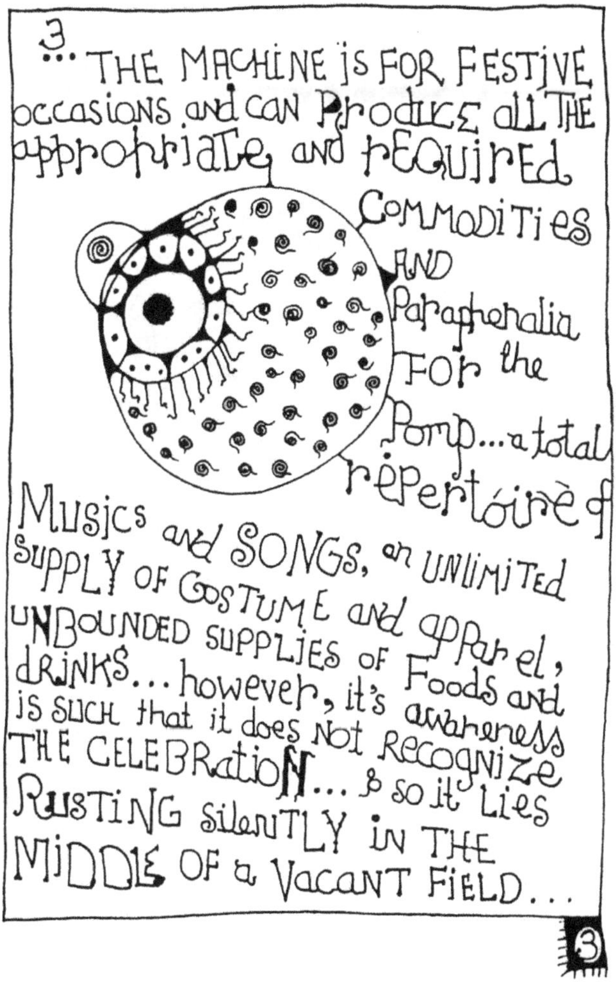

3... THE MACHINE is FOR FESTIVE occasions and can produce all THE appropriate and REQUIRED COMMODITIES AND Paraphenalia FOR the Pomp... a total repertoire of Musics and SONGS, an UNLIMITED SUPPLY OF COSTUME and apparel, UNBOUNDED SUPPLIES OF Foods and dRINKS... however, it's awareness is SUCH that it does NOT RECOGNIZE THE CELEBRATION... & so it Lies RUSTING silently IN THE MIDDLE OF a VACANT FIELD...

3

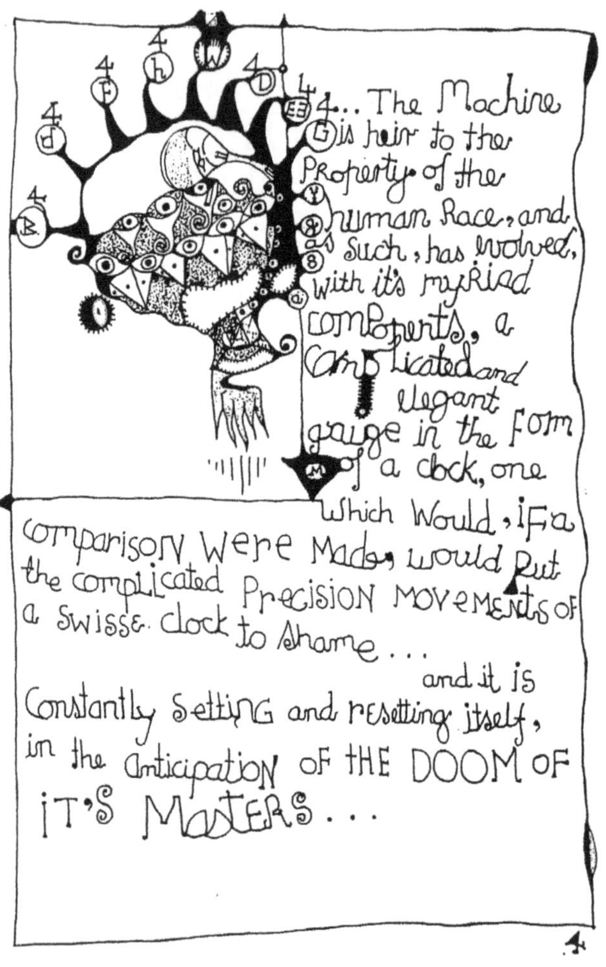
4... The Machine is heir to the Property of the human Race, and as such, has evolved, with it's myriad components, a complicated and elegant gauge in the form of a clock, one which would, if a comparison were made, would put the complicated Precision movements of a Swisse clock to shame...
and it is constantly setting and resetting itself, in the anticipation of THE DOOM OF IT'S MASTERS...

...the machine is a (canopied) seat on the elephant's thick-skinned back, only the elephant has died in his tracks and is now a mummy giving sustenance to a host of myriad creature-life and as each peeling flake of mummified hide falls from the elephant, the MACHINE emits a scream which has the character of a swarm of over-sized red butcher-ants caught-up struggling amid the taut strings of a Philharmonic orchestra

6

…THE Machine of Perpetual MOTion
defies description, however, somewhere
in it's inert core are lying the past,
the Present, and the future, and
this trio are involved in a
ProFligacy,
with open gaping jaws and
Rampant GeNitalia that is 'PREGIS',
so competent to the point of cold-
bloodness and for Which there is
NO PREhensiLiTy……

6

·7·

The MACHINE is largely conceived of bizarre INSECT FORMS, WHICH having been cast in the Goldsmith's Shop bear SOMETHING of his avarice... IF ONE Moves close to the MACHINE FOR the Purposes of inspection, a gong loudly RESounding, Resounds, and the the INSECT then BEGIN to DEVOUR Eachother in a furore, leaving, in the END, ONLY ONE LARGE Shining auriferious INSECT iridescent With the smile of digestion...
(the machine's owner is then required to send his messenger-boy to the gold-smith's for replacements...)...

⑦

(A)

The Machine is used Solely for excecutions, and contained therein on black STEEL WALLS displayed with all pre-EMINENT grace as in the Sancity of a MUSEUM are all the devices of the TRADE, and as each member of the human Race awaits, Singularly, in PROLEPSIS up on the dimpled IRON Ramp, there comes the Regular Sounds (with accompanying intervals) of the Machine's function function being Satued...

!

(8).

9

...THE Machine is of a ruthless CONSISTENCY, FOR it Produces articles again and again and again to the Same^2 Design, in the same colours, of the same weight and fashion, and in the same irreparable manner, Ruthlessly.

...however, the articles it's production enshoes are all unique, are all individual, for the machine with it's thoroughness and totality marks, scars, each article with the profundity of itself; trade mark, trade-name, patent, Place of Manufacture, etc.,, and in doing so, ensures that each such article is struck in it's own base image...

9.

10.

21...

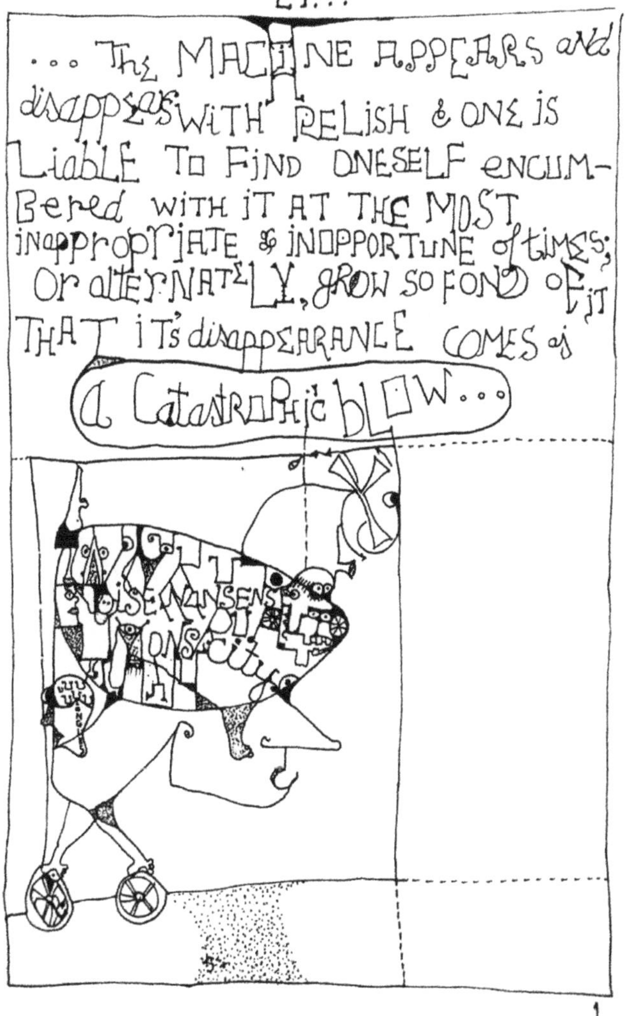
... The MACHINE APPEARS and disappears WITH RELISH & ONE IS Liable To FIND ONESELF encum-Bered WITH IT AT THE MOST inappropriate & INOPPORTUNE of times; Or alternately, grow so fond of it THAT it's disappearance COMES as
a Catastrophic blow...

1.

The Skull

a story

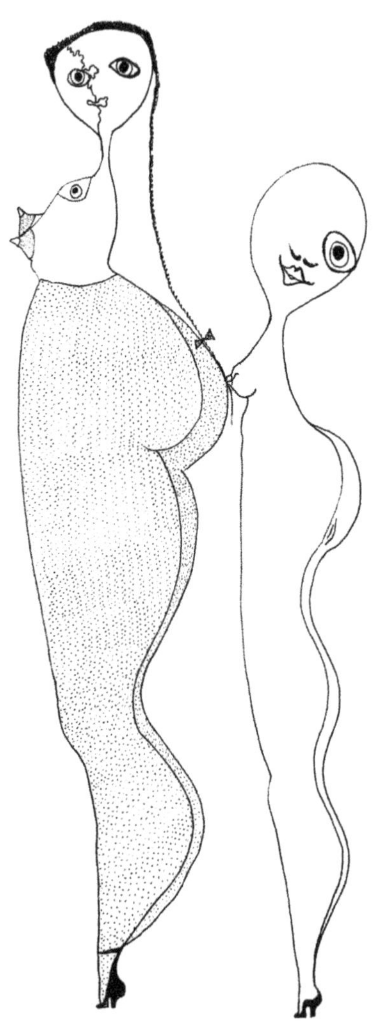

For Melissa

At the still point of the turning world.
Neither flesh nor fleshless;
Neither from nor towards;
at the still point, there the dance is …

T. S. Eliot

Cease not to think of the Universe as one living Being, possessed of a single Substance and a single Soul; and how all things trace back to its single sentience; and how it does all things by a single impulse; and how all existing things are joint causes of all things that come into existence; and how intertwined in the fabric is the thread and how closely woven the web.

Marcus Aurelius

THE SKULL * THE SKULL * THE SKULL * THE SKULL

! For a while The Head was a piece of wood, but it was pretending a masquerade … and then little black moons like trapdoors crept open & those eyes started to growl and stare violently at my feet which on its own world, in its own territory is/are possessed by the Enemy; & these eyes, they ran with a hatred like gigantic waterfalls in a trickle & in Reason which was like an insect made into bone. The Bone of The Head. Cockroaches were in its eyes and I fell in Love with them

and …

! The Head was gone. I looked because I had been staring straight at it.

THE SKULL * THE SKULL * THE SKULL * THE SKULL

! The Moon was in The Head but this was wrong because the bone was too dirty, but it was like the moon born dead and rotting and erotic but this was wrong because The Moon was big & open & moist in The Sky … it was like The Head was made from a shit of the moon.

! The Head could not spit at me as it wanted to for it had not the lips only small plates of bone and its eyes stank it was so vexed that it didn't have the necessary device to propel the spit at me and so I saw that The Head did not really know itself although it was quite possible, quite probable that it knew it had not lips. I was quite surprised when the spit ran down its chinbone and was dripping on the ground for I saw it was a most bright green like tart apples …

and again …

THE SKULL * THE SKULL * THE SKULL * THE SKULL

! I was looking at the eyes of The Head & The Eyes which I had fallen in love with which were like black cockroaches, silenced, forever, were gone and in their place were swirling corkscrews boring at a silver storm and I looked down because they made me feel cold and on the ground were two broken cockroaches & they were being devoured by red ants and it occurred to me very quickly and lightly like a kiss that I was coming to know The Head and it me …

! … if The Skull could have it would have laughed but it could not because it had not voice but instead it looked deeply into its left and I did as it did & looked to my left and looked deeply and I saw that It was looking into its imagination and not imagining

! Our eyes came back again like moths in the night and for a moment I realized that The Head's eyes were identical, in every way, always, but then I saw this Thought.

THE SKULL * THE SKULL * THE SKULL * THE SKULL

! Something began to talk in my Sleepe, something began to talk in the black airs inside my head … in The Black Place where it is like a frozen stomach … where it is a joyous place … where it is a black place … where little specks of light are eaten by the darkness. This beginning of talking was most strange because in this black place there has not been talking or sound, not even the beginning of talking … at first it couldn't comprehend … it was not like sound at all, if anything it was like Thought. The stops & starts of the sound were like mercury metals and they ran wet but dry, warm but not living, without legs around the warm walls of the wet place, The Black Place. They made the airs cold and then showed themselves angrily as thousands of silver lights like fat slugs. I began to drown. I felt sick. There was a crack like a piece of thin glass or mirror breaking & now for the first time I saw that The Black Place had floor, had limit, and on this floor was a luminous body very small which was what was left of the quick joy of the place & slowly I woke to the sound of an angry voice in my head and after shaking The Voice to dust and feeling my limbs and their stiff life I looked to The Head. I was slow in my thought because of the dissolving sleep and because of the little creature of change that was crawling and hurting my skin because it had been put there by The Head because now The Head had lips. The lips moved at me like moving wet cloth that contains something. I did a small dance in the air of the morning and seeing a shovel dug a small hole in the ground in honour of The Skull now possessing lips,

then …

THE SKULL * THE SKULL * THE SKULL * THE SKULL

! when I had finished digging the little hole I felt strangely and the hot-bright mammal of the morning rolled upon its back and fell asleep & the fleshy breeze that came made its iridescent fur into a hallucination and turned the smile on my lips bad, sour, and there was a small smell that was unpleasant & for a moment I felt to pluck down The Head and bury it in the Hole, but this feeling went and it was afternoon.

! I went to sleep for a short time in the summer of the afternoon. As I was to fall quietly away I opened my eyes and looked at The Skull. It seemed to be in itself & asleep, or perhaps in a thought, it looked erect as if there was a spine that was making itself very straight inside of it. I had a little thought that was like a drunken summer insect and that was to rise up & kiss the skull. I went to sleep with a slow, drugged smile upon my lips. Once, before becoming completely asleep I imagined that my moustache was a fuzzy-fat caterpillar.

THE SKULL * THE SKULL * THE SKULL * THE SKULL

! As I slept I was sleeping in myself; then I began to dream. The Head came out onto a stage; there were musicians & theatre lighting; & a small luminous body to give The Head mobility. The Head began to tap-dance, it would stop and bang a cane against its black-silk-top-hat & look to me & I would applaud feverishly, the joys rising inside of me like a thick incense. The dream never finished nor journey'd for I found myself no longer looking at the hat of black silk, but now closed looking at the black of the night finding the stars like blind men …

! The Head was very entertaining … it would look down from the rough wooden beam on which it was and be most extraordinary in itself … anyone would have seen that it was being extraordinary and would have been immediately transfixed, like myself, but what It was doing or not doing was unknown, was indefinable.

Today

! I put my first question to The Head; it was the first time I spoke to It also. I thought to catch it quickly so that I could move, so that I could move on elsewhere, so that I need not be where It is.

! The Skull is infinite, like the hallucination, only moreso, because it is not a hallucination.

THE SKULL * THE SKULL * THE SKULL * THE SKULL

! The Skull has been changing in size very slightly, oscillating. If I was not myself defined nor bound by the expression of definition, I would call it 'orbiting'.

! The Skull is changing all the time in size, slightly, but is not going in a direction, is ultimately getting no bigger or no smaller. But this change, now that I have seen It is like a music, a music that is made on a big, pure silver & fine instrument; a music that is of water as if planets were revolving & orbiting in water. This is most strange because I would say, now that The Head's element is fire and there is not anything about it that reflects light; not Its sweat making on It beads which do so because of the sun or the moon, because It never sweats …

! … at first I did not know the changing, I thought perhaps that it was some fallacy in my eyes to see The Skull different sizes when I looked but I tested my eyes with other things that were and they did not change size to my eyes. So then I knew it was The Head & then I knew It was a music.

THE SKULL * THE SKULL * THE SKULL * THE SKULL

! After many hours I fell into the heat which was sleeping because it was night and because it was black. Before the weight of my body fell into my body I had already begun to see into a dream. The Head was close to me & I began to expand; soon I would be increased in size enough to put out my hand and touch it, perhaps hold It, with the fingers of my hand. I did not want this to happen. I did not want to touch The Skull. I became inside a great black fear that twisted as if it was injured & which walked as if it was part of a bat, part of a man. When my fear became moist & I was about to cry out, when my fingers were as close as a tiny insect to The Skull, then I would begin to shrink away from The Skull and there was some great pain inside this thing because despite the terror, I wanted greatly to take The Skull in my fingers and why, I did not know. In all of this, which happened again & again and seemed always original, The Skull made no expression or gesture & pretended that it was dead.

THE SKULL * THE SKULL * THE SKULL * THE SKULL

! When I awoke I found The Skull was bigger. But also was the beam of wood on which it was, and the hole and the shovel and the ground. Either my eyes were different or my size was smaller and since nothing would change any longer not even in dream, I was slowly lost in a speculation with many arms and many legs but without a face.

! The face of The Head is as if familiar to me … I have just recognised it. It is like the memory of a friend that has drowned in the moving grey sands in my mind & that is now buried beneath a dune and even the dune would be an impossibility to locate, to look at the face to see if it is my friend, to see if it is The Skull, & in seeing The Head familiar, all other things have become familiar and I find this more disconcerting than if they had lost their indifference.

THE SKULL * THE SKULL * THE SKULL * THE SKULL

! … I have just been observing The Head without it observing me. I did not think this possible without It observing me also – the situation has always been as such from the first. I noticed The Skull. It occurred to me, quickly, to deepen the small hole I had dug in the ground so that it would contain my entire torso, leaving only my head showing. The Skull would not look for this, not notice only a head … it would be too much like looking for itself.

!! The Head has been here for some time now and is no more familiar to me than when it first became apparent. Neither has it become any more of the alien than when it first became apparent. This stasis seems unusual but I do not know why.

THE SKULL * THE SKULL * THE SKULL * THE SKULL

!! It rained forcefully today. The bone of The Head stood against the gun-blue sky like a monument, a monolith. I stared continuously at it, in an unbroken gaze and It at me also, as the rain made a great long noise upon the tin roof. Never before have I known a hate such as there was for no reason, nor seen such a beauty in it. At last The Skull became an apparition to me; as a ghost; dream.

!! From the onset I felt myself prepared, but now I wonder if I have not made a fundamental error in judgement. I had estimated The Head to be quite different from myself. To be of a different order, internally, and have acted and maintained myself towards The Head according to this premise. I wonder if the differences are so great and the similarities so little? Could not the reverse be quite possible? I am disappointed in thinking thus, for I suspect it means The Skull has an advantage upon me now and I do not know any of the structure within which the advantage is to be used, assuming that it exists.

THE SKULL * THE SKULL * THE SKULL * THE SKULL

!! Practically, my mind has instructed me to turn this disadvantage (if it exists) into advantage, but the lines of thought I must think to do so have become so elongated and distended and elastic, that I am weary. With this effort in mind I woke with a start to find The Head intently gazing at me, moving its lips.

!! The Head affected me adversely for the first time, last night. It was in the form of a potent & horrific nightmare. I do not embody It with … power to affect any other than myself. Another might find it entertaining or of The Absurd. I find this view puts the experience somewhat within the competence of the philosophical & somewhat less disagreeable …

!! The nightmare has become repetitive & in substance is identical with each occurrence. The Head is in the nightmares so greatly that it has put me into a turmoil that is like a fever and in this state the shadows of connotation, I feel as if I am slowly drowning in the sweat made by this fever ....
....

The Demise

The moon excretes
and a double-headed snapping-turtle comes upon it and to devour itself devours this intoxicant, and explodes – to the cloud I offer nothing but congratulations – the moon bleeds into the night and in the town 227,569 people have orgasms. I have nothing to offer, again, but congratulations – we are breeding the inhabitants to de-mystify wonders. The process is the cold snake of ice that wriggles up my arsehole. It bites deep and makes me sniff and howl at the moon. It makes me want to devour my own flesh. I have smelt the scent of Horus. Of the Underworld, of the sun that lurks in the subterranean. I am infected with the rustle of leaves that will turn into corpses if not watched. With doppelganger that appear, and leer. And turning one step to their right will again disappear. They seem to suck all music into their guts. They makc a history in my mind. They kill Sound. Things breed coldness from the ice that is they. They occur mostly along the long, polished black road where definition is, if not outlaw, at least suspect and transient. There is room there for a variation that hacks blindly at the veins that chews without any discrimination that gulps down a life and cares not what will have to be digested by the system. In all these places I have found pieces of myself. And the collection is always becoming more complete and more becoming and more macabre. There are lights among the exhibits and I am one of them. I suspect that I am in two – that I am an exhibit also. My blood is too

warm to be singular. In my repertoire I have account to the mystic places, to the FELT. The hairs of these beasts are rough and tearing against my flesh and the sheer power causes blood to come out of my nose. I am captive to the noise and it is only recently, after hearing it for years that I come to know that I, myself have been making it. I search for any mark to orientate but everything has been dug over again and again as if there walks in front of my life the spectre brandishing a broom of skulls. The furrows in the path I tread connote such a thing. I have to devour the earth to cross it.

I am continually calling upon the Gods, and they keep appearing but with different names; different cataclysms and knowing them is like knowing heat in all its wonder – the flames that have poured from me in these 32 years sear the physical material around me. I am careful not to change this reality, at least not too quickly. It will be noted somewhere 'hallucination', 'psychosis', dementia, but still the names choked in the throat. I am perpetual. The motion I engender seems to me a grinding, grinding – the grain must be ground to flour, but in this instance it is not grain but bone and they are most desiccated to begin. God can only pray for the product of this darked and brittle-legged industry. I wish to purchase myself, but the price is far in excess of anything I had previously contemplated. I am cold in the stomach. There is the balance there, and the scales, and the ruthless. I have sold myself to every possible demise but I still lived. I wonder if and regularly that I am not the walking sacrifice that am I not totally incompetent in the art of self-slaughter. Can I not rid myself of myself? The black eyes always haunt and the man I met was telling me his theory. It seems the black eyes are destiny. But why should it be offered like cold spittle? Heats and ices abound inside of me like plagues. I am sworn to knowledge and every step to it is like a mania built from the trees – only the trees scream, bite, hiss, bear names such as apoplexia, epilepsy, what is my fate to be lost within this forest? I welcome the change that will strip away the colours with which

I comfort myself to see the reality. The face. The knowledge. The music one hears becomes very familiar, I assure you. I take the tiny fires, those intimate of myself and blaze myself to ashes. It is like serving a God. It is. The Daemon has pronounced me one of his, and I have devoured him nonchalantly in some back room with the lights glued to my brain. If I have a song to sing, it will be very, very crude. For this is a circle of hell and I am occupied with it. Can I touch you lightly? Can I say of myself? The plots I have intrigued are many and confusing. Do we not all wish some form of cold-blooded slaughter to free us? I have thought as much. Think carefully, the circle you draw in the dust becomes magic in the night – and eats into the flesh. If there is a hell it is that I have not intruded far enough. That I am stuck in the uterus still and am choking. I mistake liberation for a life without pain. I wish to burn now, for how else is the penumbra changed? Give to me the taste of charcoal remnants. I defy. And yet the truth of these things keeps me afloat. If I could assault with deadly violence my soul I would do so. We are on such terms.

I shake like a leaf and in using the 'simile' become the leaf and must fight. The words I hear around me are deadly potent. If I could wield the thought like solid matter how much would I destroy and how much would I make? I want to see the madnesses expounded for how else are these unborn children that one sees in the plethora of beings to be laid to earth quietly, quickly and with the appropriate ceremony? I look to the night sky and in seeing it see the Other. A thousand black, miniature crucifixes adorn the night and on each one a child's doll is nailed, brutally. They bleed and I know not what. In this night which is a desert I am alone. Perhaps there is too much. Perhaps we should, cut from, take for, select part of, make divisible such, but time seems to be armed and the daggers hack deeply. Why is it that there is so little noise? I look to the paper and see a female suicide. My blood runs cold. The threads of the plot seem to grasp like steel. I am an adept at horror and liberation. If I could tell you the secrets I know you would look twice, perhaps thrice to see who I am. I can only tell you that the world tastes rusty. Its shine is gone. Inside of the cradle we no longer have children. We are brewing the concoction. And when it comes time to drink, we'll all choke. The darkness is expanding. I talk to him again of the supreme being. How can it lay not cogito across such tongues as ours? Surely it is hungry and wishes to devour? But the questions seem to run like blood down a wall. I bath in it regularly. I adorn myself with bloods thinking myself in the credit. Only to find that they are my bloods alone and they trickle through my fingers. In my sleep I hunt with a dagger. What I have killed and maimed I hang around my neck and am weighted by. I sometimes find it difficult to move away from the stench of catastrophe. Why I should collect the unstable I do not know. It devours my limbs – I am not outcast because I can be flung no further. I do not wish to find out the nature of the stains on my hands. Why must I inspect and define my own bloods, my own breath, my own beginning? To all those that listen, I do not talk, I shout. Have you felt the vacuum? It is impure, imperfect – it leaks and that is the first and last sound I hear in the days – a trickle of liquid. What it can be I hesitate to speculate. In this world of mechanical sounds I expound the organic, the trickle and murmur of liquids through the stomach, thru the intestines. For they are the only ones in which we can drown and begone. The others only reflect, wash, insinuate. The knife is in my friend's pocket and I am brought to wonder what might be its future. Will someday soon it not be used against me? I question all about it. As I touch myself I hear the screams, the interspaces, the sentences of all those that have touched me. Why should it be so? What am I to them? My very nature seems to run on the ground between my legs and carve a living delta out of the earths. I squat and examine these. I am too lost in the speculation of the beautiful form to enquire with any power where the lifebloods came for this construction. The corner is. And in knowing one corner it comes to pass that nothing is hidden. If my knowledge is correct I am sitting on a bomb and cannot even discern that I am seated. I am smothered. The Irreal. The Dream. The Real. Psychosis. Mania. Loss. The adventure of mistake. They are all like a beast around me. It tears the flesh – but instead of devouring it does else – it brings to the boil. It makes apparent. All runs together and the legs stifle. The noise of the thoughts and messages coming to me deafen. They cannot be separated. They almost lunge as if they themselves are homicidal and lost on The Strange Road. I am lost to all beginnings. There is the decided attempt to affiliate with an ending and I am taken in trance by this. The woody knots of a gnarled life are difficult to carve. Would that I had collapsed at birth into a more complete form – one where the definition is not treated like poison. One where every noise is not a scream and without the common name. I tire people with the analogy. They see scream again and again on paper and are not impressed. I have not the wit to offer fancy alternatives. Besides, this affair is what occurs. If I could burn down myself I would begin immediately gathering combustion. The same symbols appear again and again and I run from them. They follow in front and grimace. Soon we will expect each other in some rapport or common manner. When I type it seems I am typing in blood. In bloods. I have become like the constructivist machine. I operate. I am efficient. But I betray for I wish to destroy. And I am dangerous for I do not know wholly what it is I wish to destroy. If I do not succeed there is penalty. I will be taken and asked. The questions already are torturing me. For I know no semblance between them and the language. They are manifest and seem to spew from the earth in a volcano. The clouds gather and the greys burn. And the ash burns the tongue. I have committed so many fallacies in my life that I wonder – for many of them have stood upon legs (some most unfirm) and accompanied me at least part of the distance. The nights come again and again. It appears that the blackness whispers of somethings unknown. I am intoxicated by it. Where is it? What is it? That we know who we are is gross premise. I wish to look over the fences into my other self. But they are at most extreme odds with each other and avoid. Perhaps they cannot stand the stink of each other. Matter and anti-matter. I would like to witness the holocaust made by their meeting. I know I would enjoy this. I have always been transfixed by flame. And yet it seems for me that all illumination and satisfaction in it has deserted and I am left with a primordial molecule which I must harvest and know not how. There is none to instruct. The journeys I have taken have always led to the most dense. I seek the intense. And in finding it am struck down. For thus it is so. Such a thing does happen often. The injuries all become ulcers. The bad foods do nothing for the healing. I am awash amongst the magnificence. It has come at last. Perhaps this desert of the UFO? Where is Jung? They land again and again in my head. They deposit. They withdraw. Why did I not use the thread when it was offered? Arrogance? Fear? Love? Again and again the Cosmos calls and I am ever ready to get it. Even though it dribbles like a performed whore. I bury my head between its legs and am safe for the moment. In my travels I find even the pebbles that inflict injury precious. I come upon a fossil rock. It is of a woman's vagina. I throw it over my shoulder and pray. But the differentiation for travel has disseminated. I no longer see the borders I no longer see the checking stations. All is travel and all is rich. If I could I would invite you with me but I fear what you think of me. Isis might send down her spittle just as easily as her blessings. There is murder in my heart so be careful not to hold my hand too tightly. It appears that the harvest is continual. That I must reap myself continuously. That I must gather the crop – and give to those their subsistence. I know not what I see. I am lost in the canyons of the desert without Yahweh. Where is the water? I am on fire and curse the name. And rightly so for he has left me in this demise. Bring forth the plagues for even these would nourish, would satisfy. I am in love with the vision of crawling on all fours like some sad Assyrian and devouring green frogs from the hind to the head. I would be looked after, attended, coiffured. Give me sustenance, O desert and no longer drive me down.

I am all angles and straight lines. The curves have deserted, have been struck from myself. I was in the woods in winter and suffered the harsh reality of fire, ice, water and cold. Now in spring the colours are rising. A thousand coloured fungi sprout from my cranium. I see light and chant and sing. The resurrection has taken place. I see the vision. I have made gently love to it underneath trees and with the wine bottle. O eccuryuubiccal, O all evil come as my guardian from the depths and sing with me. Incant the Satanic Principalities and grow. They haunt me in the wonder. They come through the hollow hole of joy in my cranium through the fissures in the skull-bone and sing and their singing is bliss. I wish it night after night. It is the music. If I am found on my knees do not be sceptical for I truly know what I am doing. When arising and looking to the sky I see a mouth in hysteria. It is like the first and the final night. I could wish for no more than a vision. By what right do we demand? By what right have we to say the vision must be this or must be that? There is no guardian upon the door so we must be ready to receive all visitors and visitations. There is wealth and it can be counted by the scars. And each is. That is the reality. That is the manifesto. I look to my waking form and am most critical. But again I use the definitions as I wish. What is waking? I am in a room. The lights change to a glow. The room seems to fill with a fragrant smoke and I speak to apparitions. The irreal twisted itself into a corded snake in my innermost guts. It is like the calling. There are those that come and go and there is no such thing as an invitation list. All are expected. Any and all appear. In my dreams I am descending stairs. I journey through the animal and am newly exited. Where and what way to horror? For it seems now so familiar to me as to be a lover. What greater thing could you reserve for your caresses? The reek and odour of my visions is extraordinary. I laugh at Ovid wishing to be all nose. I wish to be all eye. TO SEE. I leave my friend who is insane and venture into the waters. But he sees molten metals and will not venture to bath. Perhaps this is best for someone will need be present and sober for the collection of my body after it smoulders to charcoal. What a mistake it was to be. For now I am a hopeless addict at its increase. Now I starve for the addition to myself. I wish to be big. I wish to fill the room – to overflow out the windows and increase still more. To fill the world. I am the bodhisattva that became wise on the floor of the insane asylum. I pray to myself and the silence when I stop is like hell. Where can such a silence come from? It is extraordinary. It must come from the insides of the monster. No other explanation will suffice. I must make an offering at the Temple of the Dog. I invoke Nemesis and Denizen; I pray to them both and gargle the prayers to the Temple of the Dog. I find the dog has begun. I cannot turn to drugs for I have found myself already partly distilled and very, very potent. I might mistake myself for a narcolepsian. I look again and in the Dog's eyes (one should say 'DOG') I see the black moon as a belly with a knife in it and the scream somehow on the dog's lips and turned into a smile. The gryphon, both of them, sit upon the weight that is the mystical, the carnal. I jest. I mania. "They are 64,000,000 years old." "They are emphatic and fragmentary and fellatic." They are mania and hysteria. They are the dried gizzards that strangle my soul. The wall of faces burns into my eyes. I fear my face might be added to the collection, resume, selection. I think this wall has come directly from the pineal gland. I scratch and curse when I am near it and wonder if it does not cause me to live in a bygone age. To not live in the furrier moments of evolution. When I am exhausted I lay down and even then are defied peace. The screeching of birds of reptiles from the cretaceous era shatter the silence upon which I was floating.

I am haunted by the ghosts of beautiful women. I have taken them all as my lovers and they shared me. Yet they still put the horrors thru me. Those of these that are the eternal suicides I cannot cope with they drive me from myself. I shake and tremble inside from their touch. And yet it is still love. And yet again to touch the irrational face of beauty is what I feel I have a predilection for. I wonder through the worlds of myself and lie that I have a knowledge in dangerous event to escape. None exist. At best I will be destroyed with myself. What oddments, what scopophilia, what splendid errata. I shrink beside them and they are so little that I scream my prayers into the pissoir of the universe. Soe and Scculio and Scooule have all taken possession of me. It was sworn that my soul would not be negotiable a second time. Someone lied.

I drive the blade of my imagination across myself and feast on the result. I am I. I cannot exceed myself. This makes me delirious. I think of one thousand gestures I have performed and burst into hysteria and total humour. It is as if my diet was nitrous oxide. They are knocking continuously for me and I am forever answering the door to let them in. I am asleep in the wilds. A car comes upon me. The driver gets out and fires several shots to where I am laying. As I am struck by the bullet I know everything of him. It is like the most intimate of exchanges. Like ritual. I am entranced into a different realm. The bardo of consciousness flows around the pain. I let a cry to the world. It sounds so powerful in my ears and so puny in the world's great cacophony. I see God's face come upon the ground and it is like an immense hot-air dirigible. I am in danger of being crushed to death by an eyeless mirage. O spare me great God. If he keeps it up I will adorn the lips with lipstick and put rouge on the cheeks. I am informed there are those who would change His sex. Good luck to them. I am sick of adoring the all-powerful; send me the luscious the Mother. I am in a café. My friend of two minutes is talking of the Mother. I tell him to beware. He tells me to beware. Such it is. I have exited the doors of the insane asylum a dozen times. And each time to find that the unreality of the said world is catastrophic and a lie. I have gone to the train station and fallen in love with motion and the singular beauty of the train-machine and only exited the rail after a week.

With beard and the well-earned kilometre's sweat. The sound of rail is like the humming of a lover's head upon my chest and fills me. Makes me whole. Devours me. I wept when I had to get off the train, broke and with an expired ticket.

The nights spent under a single blanket in winter in the stranger parts of this city are my main qualification. If you do not think me able for the job then do not employ me, but I know. And in knowing can see you. I am unhappy with what I see. Be informed. The shaking in my limbs is not natural. How and why it is there is most enigmatic. It is as if I am shaking for the whole human race. Why should this be so? I feel when I retire as if I am going to be with four billion others. I look to the strange caves where I lived and ask them questions. Only they might answer. The lights of the past, the present and the future gleam. I have unwittingly slain Shiva. I led to destruction on the rocky paths. And now his chant starts and is like glory coloured in such reds as to be incommunicable. The slashing gongs and strings put faeces in my pants. I must run and knowing this I leave instantly creeping past His gaze. The next night and the next I return. The harsh bloods of the forest own me. In the frozen frame of morning I see the giants and all their kind. I will not discuss aliens. I have seen too much. The irreal is as if a giant snake, green and forever twisting. If I can only breathe. If I could only breathe I would consider myself fortunate. The winds of the forest are like lovers who never left. I penetrate but in doing so lose. Start the processes of decay in action. I delay. My lovers are suspicious. "I want you inside of me," I am told. But already the gesture is holding the cupped hands of a parting.

I write about the women in my life. I must and they each and en masse recriminate me. "It wasn't as such," they say. Was it as anything. This concoction that is being brewed will not quite go around. But I will not lapse into the morbid. What chance I? One single spike against the rubber plungers? What to gain? I already have enough exhaustion to last centuries. I would speak of earthquakes but it is no mean thing that when such is happening we all deny the earth. The earthquake is most unsettling. After, the estrangement from earth is mammoth. A man comes up to me at a party and wants to know why I am shaking. Drugs? Alcohol? Nerves? I tell him it is the eternal earthquake. The crust of the universe like a scab falling off a wound. He will not talk to me any longer. I think we have relieved each other. And there was not the slightest mention or indication of sex. A woman speaks to me of puppets. I am to become a puppeteer. But I am too engrossed in taking from my limbs the myriad of strings and devices that are there for me. The only sure thing that seems to withstand the fury is dream. It somehow has such a vitality and resilience that defies all. I keep a library. I carefully alter, knead, re-enrapture myself to the point of intoxication. I am informed of 'eyelid movies' which occur before sleep but in mine the projectionist is a drunk layabout and bungles everything. What I crave is the deep colour of the subconscious and the vistas of the unconscious. The Shadow comes to be regularly and leaves footprints. In one dream he transported me to my parent's bed and using an enormous zipper interred me there. The situation brought horror. The emotions had me fighting with the walls. I can settle in front of the typewriter with far more freedom than before a woman's crotch. Why is this? Is my own vainglory so omnipotent? Decidedly, the typewriter is more demanding and the harsher tyrant. I look from my window in one of the deadest hours of the night and I see the new Gods seducing mankind. Cumfeel & feelcum & cumfelt & feltcum. A mythology grows like tropical fungi. It is with alacrity that their substance grows in my brain. Once I went out to inspect one of my gods after swearing alliance and found nothing but an overactive street light on a large wooden pole. Such, alas, is the folly. I have given my belief to the ephemeral and danced. If the dance had the beauty then it cut my throat as the finale, well what can one say? Having an artistry means having an appreciation of wonder that has no bounds. I will tell you a story. I am mad and living at a hotel in the inner city. Across the street a beauty lives and she is mostly nude when indoors. Each night after dark and when not asphyxiated with culture I stand and look at her and write her love letters in poetry. No letters or gestures are returned but then perhaps this is the sublimity in which I can make love. I will not part from the fantasy even when I cannot pay the bill for the room. What enriches is poetry. And poetry without vision is a burden. You will find that the humblest on the streets are those with the gigantic vision. It is what they administer to. They are themselves guardians. They are clothing the visions that have occurred within them by their flesh. They do this from the touch of others in all manner. Most dangerous is the theft of a vision. In the telling of it it becomes accessible and one just might put one's hand in and swipe it. Temptations about the irrational and intangible are extreme. They inhabit the illogical extremities of man's nature.

I invite calamity. It's my nature. All it takes is the slightest deviation and my life is put into chaos. I burn with distraction. With power. And yet it is a devastation for it is against me not with me. I curse the architect of the universe, everything. It could not be otherwise. In the night wherein the mists fold like sculpture and the ghosts appear I feel free. It is this strangeness, this wonder which activates my nerves. This is where I seek liberation. In the pit, the furnace of myself. Tiny alterations will cause momentous events and actions to take place. There is not the least whimsy in myself. If it was there it's a smothered child now and this leads to obsession. I have a monomania. It is to be. And nothing else. I grasp this with all my might. If I could pray for you I would but alas, all I have I need myself. I struggle, I make sound, I drown. No-one notices. Such is the plague of our times. I am in love with the wine. "All the more," "Keep it rolling," I shout. I will drink this substance life until I am so sickened by it that I expire puking. The metaphor, the analogies swarm. I have seen myself destitute. I have fed myself from the rich porcelain plate and the garbage tin. I have slept in beds of silk with wondrous women, sublime women and I have slept in the mud and stink with the noxious despair of myself trying to conquer. I jest. I lie. I say I am not broken only temporarily beaten. But the pieces that make up the trail of myself stand truthful. The realities are unavoidable. I have seen. I have seen so much that I am in a constant glut. And I want to see more. I crave the threads of life. I am the intriguer. The expressionist. I have not the time of day for the scientists. They lie away their lives. They are building structures around me that seem of the conspiracy. The industrialists I loathe. I see Krupp's face now with this reference and it is in electrolepsy and crimson. It is telling me to trust it. It is the old story. I have had them. All day I have heard them bleat and chant for my vote. I despise them. I vote for MYSELF. No other action is possible. The wealth encapsulated inside the mortal defies the sham of the graven images they present. At the lunacy of the fruitless life. O do not mistake me. I know of production, output, productivity. But look closely. The fruit is bitter and not only that it is poison to boot. Better to hang bodies from the trees and claim it as labour. At least the façade would be stripped away. Beware, we are cannibals. We are so complete. I do not know for how long we have been thus but we are truly so. Take to the streets and it is plain. As an educator the desperate is magnificent. Nothing surpasses it. I have been torn and am still being torn. Sometimes I occupy my time by taking an inventory of the scars. It is wondrous how precious pain turns out to be. I am throwing down more and more cards to the floor but the deck remains. Will I ever come to the end of myself? Perhaps. I expect one day to pull apart the last petal the last fragrance and know. Alas, the journey is cruel and sick. I incant Polygr God of lusts and words. Make me clever, make me glib. Give me possessions. I will sell my soul at the slightest invitation but only on the increment system. I want a fair deal for it. It's been nurtured and cropped like the best grapes. I disagree with my dead mother who saw the experiences that I undergo depreciating the value. Every night spent cold on park benches purifies it, makes it more enticing to the valuer. I look to the crowds at train stations, bus stations, cafes, hotels, motels, for hope. Very little is given. They are glutted with bloods. An iota more calcium or magnesium and they will explode. If you were to prick them with a pin the bloods would spurt as if under tremendous pressure.

I am in love with the riffraff. Always have been. They are melted beings. Their metal is the true colour of the dark. It is without shine. There are the graven lines of pain and contemplation. Of fear and ecstasy. I stop on the street and watch the old women dance. She is exhausted but still she moves. Nothing is more like the ant and less like it. The looks of the passersby astound. It is as if joy is a disease. Viva qui vive. "Coxxo nota bombif carsa discurssa a vneral diimonds" I want to shout at them. But then perhaps it is better to gun them all down quickly and quietly against some wall. But their death would be dismal. Note how marvellous the Nazis were in the executions and expirations during intrigues. The fanatic decidedly knows the way to die. I feel I could raise a scythe and mow them down by the hundreds like wheat. But there is danger here also. These ants are patient. They are calculating. They believe in the order. All the same it's a hell of a price to pay for a clean beak while at the trough. Give me the feast even if it is hurried. Even if the lamb grease does get tangled up into my beard. I crave the odours. I crave the colours. And will give hell to get them. All my life it seems has been a hunt for them. I will not stand obfuscation. Give me what is mine. Give us what is ours. Let us be free of the meeknesses. They and their values were only projected so that the famine would be acceptable. I am as far from jaded as the onager from the submissive beauty. I drink at an everlasting cunt and still I desire more. The room in which I shout at you, whisper to your fantasies, cajole you, give vent, is drowning beneath the colours of all sorts of art. I stand for the wondrous creativity of the outcast who is yet the common man. He makes wonders appear before your very eyes and as if in apology puts them away after you have seen them. I have been seeking now friends and art and have come away from their vision replete and ennobled. I have been struck with lights and the motion of the emancipated mind. I have seen the clearness of love put onto thin paper and see it defy the calculation of the city in which it lives, in which it exists. I would burn a thousand museums to the ground to guard one of these pictures. Marvellous. Send me not your weak, send me your strengths; I am in need of them. Write to me of the promises that are fulfilled. It is a flame that is an agony down the backbone and up in the cranium. There are limitations to what can scratch the paper. I go over to the window and shout out and return to you. You are not so reverent that I must become your slave. I will think myself blessed by it. It is not the destroyer of a life, but the makings of it. As a schizerino all became one and that thing was mind. For how many can say they possess? Not many. The slimness of the numbers even frightens. I was able to stretch my limbs out to the horizons and all within their grasp was mine. But it is not the state, it is the wonder. The words. The dreams. The equations which always were edible, malleable, equitable, which mattered.

I have been in the storm with my friend, Fascinatio. We were both dumbstruck by its ferocity, by its beauty. Thousands of great spiders made out of polished platinum cascaded down upon the earth – the night of the holocaust of spiders. A seemingly endless array of fingers from cast green iridescent bronze showered us, blinded us – the night of swimming fingers. There were explosions. Great floods of lights and sparks – the night of Cosmic Contortions. Dear reader, I must tell you Fascinatio is in my mind. She is imaginary. She is one of the most congenial of those I have ever met in life. I am eternally wedded to her. For this incarnation and the rest. She is as much a part of me as my skull is. I know I am being intimate but I must. There is no force like her in the universe. She is the ever-changing and the constant. She is the Empress and the strumpet. She is the high-priestess and the housemaid. I know that it will not offend her to speak of her thus for I know her soul and its complexity and pluralism to the very depths. Companionship à droit. Save? The Danse de Boire. It is difficult when the most intimate in one's life is of such consistency. Do not be lulled into thinking I have a totally free hand to treat as I wish. Far from it. I must maintain myself with decorum and poise. I must espouse the virtues constantly. One slip and she challenges me. God, the oppression and the masochism and to boot the microcosm. She permeates all. Initially she was mine with which to play. Now she is as a New York mugger. She carts me off to bed the instant the clock (which is imaginary also) strikes to twelve. The whispering and giggles beneath the bedclothes have brought curious looks and comment. Dear reader what do you think of horror. "Horror is my honeybunch". I have just returned from the great garden of the mental asylum. From the insane night with the winds high in the trees and the soul of the place tremulous and foreboding. The trees are gnarled by the toothless mouth of an oppression which is unanswerable. Which is enslaving. The horrors that blow past one, one must ignore to survive. The more you notice of such an environment whilst in it the more vulnerable you become to injury. The friend I was with thought that I had walked into a gigantic spider web but it was not so. I walked into the horror of a hundred hundred madness and without a single thought prepared in my head. To say the night was occult is to be incomplete. But everywhere around and sometimes within sight the ghosts of this place were evident. Were watching us. I have just come from the darkest night I have known ever in this garden of horrors. I hid behind a tree and watched two female ghosts make a horrifying lesbian love to one another. My hair stood on end. I came as they came and I felt that I had spilt a pint of blood into my trousers. And it was true when I arrived home I found my underwear a stained crimson with the high wine of blood. I know not the difference from one world to another. Every path seems to scream at me to tread it. I have just returned from a sculptor's workshop. He tells me of the love of wood and the dignity of creative labour. The smells of his world were intoxication. The sweat and labour of each piece of fashioned wood a joy to behold. I wanted to devour them all. I wanted to buy and live within his studio. I am lost within the marvels of the human soul and know not the exit. The paths all yell and they all yell the wonder that is in their treading. How am I beset so?

I have just returned from the country. I found it God-given. The stark eyes of intelligence have been staring from the naked and most high-flung dressed night. The fragrances were a delight. I am coming to know the mute glory of the wilder parts of this country. I was shot by a psychopath whilst there. The bullet is still lodged in the left leg and I am to have surgery next week. Again it never rains but it pours. The eternal polarisation. The hand that offers also chokes. An interesting experience, you think? Why must I go all the way to the country to find my psychopath?

I am just returned from the Temple of the Dog. An eerie experience. The dog's head was put up as decoration only and to signify something which is now well and truly lost. But the Age of the Dog has taken over. In the slow slum night around it derelicts come from all places to offer their dicks for veneration and to piss below the head of the dog. In return the dog blesses their dicks and rots their livers. Someone has poured crimson/red paint into the dog's gaping mouth. I even have a picture of the dog, two. Three.

I am again thinking of my life. It has become the obsession in my life so to joke. I am thinking most of those times of being a derelict and living on the streets. The eternal slogging from one place to another in the cold. The bedding down on building sites and in graveyards. The intelligence one gains on the might that is the city is almost beyond mention. When one knows it as thus one is truly in awe of it. One realises the city as a living thing. A thing that has gained the presence of animation, intelligence, cognisance, call it what you will. In this mood, in this humour, one exceeds the Suicide so that one has no place for it in one's life. It is the process of purification that forces the feet from one spot to another. From the spleen of the city right to its glittering pineal gland. I have sat musing on train stations and seen great cities appear on the horizon and seduce me and seduced I have been by their glory. I have gone down and knelt to them and prayed for them to come to me to open their doors so that I may enter their citadels. That I might penetrate as a tiny generating sperm and make them fecund and rich with myself. And the visions have passed. But not without the grace of the vision staying with me. Not without the breathless revelations. I have been visited by apparitions that have informed me of the secrets and the occult. They whisper and chant and give thought and speculations. More than one night I have sat in the public gardens illegally and attended to these visions and learned of the esoteric. The problem disappears when one is so taken by the muses the genii. I find myself walking the street rubbing my crotch instead of the lamp trying to conjure up God knows what. And it has been successful. I have conjured up everything. I doubt that the novel exists. I doubt that there is a single apparition or knowledge that I have not placed my lips to and drunk and whispered thanks to and prayed to and have been struck by. I have been to the bed of the sea and pulled the plug from the ocean's floor. I have wandered in the sun and picked strange protozoic fish out of the mud that remained and examined them. I have trod the unimagined underfoot as if it was nothing and have felt it bite into my feet. I have stood eye to eye with the twisted, warped, the truly distorted and have spoken to it and it to me. I have stared into fountains and seen bodies swirl about locked in a majesty of the carnal beyond contemplation and then the whole shebang has collapsed into a puddle of piss at my feet. The winds of karma which drive me are their own purpose. I will not question them. I will not speak of the knowledge. It is there and this is enough. It will one day lead me through the chaos and out into eternity. I long for the day but

I will not prompt it or pre-empt it. It will come as surely as death. And it may very well be accompanied with a death. I will not jest with something such as this. I am just returned from the bathroom and a suicide attempt. I took the kitchen carving knife and filled the bath to the brim with warm water and immersed my flesh and bared the knife. But the holocaust left me and like an idiot I found myself with the knife and useless. But I am freed from whatever drove me to this desperation. It drowned in the water. Its heart lies carved up and bloody in the toilet. And floats among the turds. Not a bad half hour's work, eh? What am I doing, dear reader? Are you still with me? I am trying to tell you of the life I have been living. I am not sure if you are still there but in the off chance that you are I will continue.

I have known joys in my life. I have wished many times not to be hedonist but to have what the hedonist is depicted as having. The debauch. The rites of Dionysus. The pell-mell scamper through the flesh, the grape, the drug, the waste. But also I have loved the Stoic. The Discipline and the Order. I am dragged to all those that enlighten. I have wasted my years in discussions with the impure who do not know, but the paradox is, in doing so I have learnt. I have been imbued and have prospered. I drown in the graveyard that is my experiences. They flash through my mind like rebellious neutrons and all yell for recognition, for space. I wish to make them into order, to be able to live with them. They demand so much of me that I am at a loss and I weep at this.

I am newly returned from a friend who lives at a mental hospital, in one of its wards. He cut his leg off because God told him to do it. Now he hobbles around on one leg and is with God. In addition he keeps sacrosanct the art of poetry and the gentle metaphor. He tells me stories and I feel that he is giving me riches, wealths. He talks of the little things of nature and love and I find myself weeping afterwards from joy. I wish to be more open. I wish to take the carving knife and carve open my flesh so that all that is, that is, might penetrate and reach the temple. That the sparks might fire instead of being extinguished in the dirt and muck. I wish for more life. I wish to build and build even though I know that in the building is destruction. I wish to touch the black monolith that I see in my mind that hums, that quivers that is like the cunt of cunts, that; holds every smell, that holds every sight, that knows every sound that will free me. I have been doing nothing in my life except removing the chains and healing I want to prosper. Oi, Rolo toxics mucka mer. Give me the power. Give me the sword. Give me the compassions and the lights. I am in the desert and all about me is the fire of the purity. I wish to remain here forever. I wish to become part of the desert. I wish to cut from my body all the canker and growths and be one with the pure desert. I am husk and inside a raging turbine. I wish to harvest the crop. To make the bread of life.

I am seething with life. Living things are spurting out from my ears. My tongue is a virtual menagerie. All my body and soul is aglow with the confluxous abound of the moving, the breathing, the thinking, and everything that I do only increases this situation. I am aglow and so it should be. I can ask for no more. I should wish for no more. Every direction has me placed in a position where a thousand more addiments, condiments, accompaniments come. The state of duplicity has long since passed into an extraordinary multiplicity. I know not the reason or reasons why my life has passed into this conflagration. Meanwhile, those insidious who have contact with me complain of my confusion, my reticence, my procrastinations. They hardly know. They do not see. I have just been in my imagination and am visibly shaken. I am awake and violently so. I am so wired up that any more added voltage will blow every fuse out of my head. Like a long stream of electronic vomit. I am thinking of the street and with cold shudders. I don't wish to end up living in the streets any more. It is a grinding experience.

The exacerbation of the soul. I give a shudder, as I say, even to remember the days when I was given the streets as my only sanctuary, my only reprieve from the chaotic structure of my life. God be praised that there was at least somewhere, although these bitumen and cement reprieves were closer to the damned bardos of existence than I care to think about. For weeks I fed myself from other peoples' refuse from their garbage, their wastes. The motivations being that any other form of life was too fraught with traps and dangers to pursue. For months the endless slog around the city penniless and ferocious paid no dividends, no compensations, excepting that the freedoms were glorious and the penalitudes and restrictions of modern life were so obvious as to be a physical presence. It is like rubbing and re-rubbing the same sore. But as I say, one can achieve a view splendid in its sheer horror and depression, in its malefaction and dismalness of what modern, ordered, life is about. I have a vision in my craw that won't leave. I think of the antiseptic city-ite and I think of a line by Henry Miller – 'wan, like a masturbator in the dark'. The Swiss clock is alive and well, AND growing. Soon there will be a place for us all in it. Eccentrics to the left please and then INTO the mechanism. Those normal or pretending so for their reasons up front, ACHTENSION. Along will come a glorified dunny-cart man pretending to be the secular gods we pray to, Mr Dollar, Mr Security, Mr Pretence and he'll wheel the whole she-bang right over the edge and good riddance. I would like to place bombs in the city, I have dreamt as much. To blow the thing, mind you I say THING, to bits to literally level it. To show off its filthy and blood-soaked underpants.

And why stop? If you are game to blow up a bank, be game to blow up the pernicious idol of the dollar with it. The vehicle that creates famines and makes a hard situation even harder. Stuff a stick of dynamite up the asshole of the International Monetary Fund. Up the orifice of the National Budget. If you are game to blow up a police station be game to blow up the whole repressive system of surveillances and impeachments upon human rights and dignity. If you are game to blow up a church get the Almighty, blow his duds off. Reduce Him to the pile of wondrous stale soup that He has always been.

Of course we ARE being radical. Of course we ARE being anarchistic. But where else are we to go? What is the worth of the individual soul? Tear the inscription off the church wall and make a placard of the thing. A motto. A daily regimen. Give us our bread and don't leave us staring with our noses squashed on the plate glass windows watching you stuff fine cakes and pastries down your throats.

I am just returned from a storm. And only now am I realizing that the storm I have been in is myself. Only now have I come to even suspect the almighty power of myself and therefore others. And the storm was from the underworld and all the old names spoke and all the mysteries were revealed. It is my fault that I was left wandering in a daze, blinded. For what was imparted was the knowledge of how to be human, truly human and it was too much. I am astounded. I look. I feel. I think. I weep. I journey and with all this there is the screaming. Look to your hinds, dear reader and you will find the footpath and pavements devouring you like a crocodile. I am just returned from the bed of the sea.

The shark is circling me and I it. It is most disturbed that I am doing just as it is but this is the only thing that I can do, it is the only thing I want to do, it is the only way I can confront it. Beware shark. Beware, I will devour you with eight foot teeth. I will spit on you and dissolve you. I will munch through your tail like a bloated prawn. And yet, strange as it may seem, in this relationship I suspect that I am in love with the shark and it with me. What is going to happen as we begin to devour each other? The onslaught is awaiting and it will reveal all.

I am just returned from prayer. I have been adding a bit of spiff and shine to the idols. They look good. I think that they are the most well cared for idols on the block. I have named them of course but then that is perfunctory as they already were named. In order from left to right is, The Irrational, The Illogical and The Irreal. They are most difficult idols and you may be forgiven for thinking me traditional and pagan but at least they give answers and the answers inspire some thought, even actions. In an age when we are giving nuts and bolts and tubes and electronic chips precedence in our life it is comforting to know that there is a little of the terrifying and terrible still left. When the computer dissolves the presence of the irrational I will call it quits. Slit open my gizzards and quietly disappear. I am much given to the presence of my idols, my pets in the human volume. They are displayed in the myriad and interlacing. They have led me into violence, fights, loves, remorses, contemplations and adventures. I know of no surrogates for them and what they are appointed to be. In what other world will a man appear as the fool and the fool appear as the man. It is trying to catch the headless chicken. The quest is ridiculous right from the beginning. I have been in the rain but I am not wet. You think me a miracle. I think myself a lunatic and vice versa. Oh Great Bob in heaven please send me some mail. Amen.

I am moved by creation and in turn move the moment to where I can reckon with it. But I am lousy and contaminated and as I have said, stuck in the desert. The scorpions chew and munch on my bones, which are falling apart from premature aging. It is true. I stuck my nose into the void as was suggested and found not the void but the Vacant, The Nothingness, The Nihilism, Zilch. I pain for the man I must meet every night before the narcotic sleep takes me, and this man is myself and not myself. Sometimes he stands over my bed and whilst I am unconscious tries to murder me. And the situation is made all the more cathartic because it must be most clear that the man is myself. And yet most clear that this man is not myself. He is more like a presence, a shadow, an apparition. Why must I labour for myself when there is either too little or too much? Every thought I think impales me through the vital organs. Through every tender thing that I possess. It is as if becoming clearer this exile. It seems. And in seeming it becomes. I cannot venture forth in my imagination for the fear that it will become the real article that it will become solid matter. The imagination that I am dealing with is that horrendous, that apocalyptic, that bizarre. Such a small thing as beauty will take me into the realms of demons of animalism, to the great waterfalls of the neurotic speculation, to the great iron floor of psychosis. I think therefore I am. And in being let loose, wild uncontrollable screams.

It is initiation, it is violence, it is vacuum, but a vacuum that leaks with blood and intestines. I am not so much the prophet as his pussy, sore-ridden feet. I am in motion and forced thus by the process. O toxicooh delicastaster ruddinth Crator. Why is it to feel so calm among the slaughter? Why is it to feel my mouth full, and my stomach empty? Why is it to be barren with a pocket full of loot? And lice? I am in contemplation now and you must leave me, but you will not. Fear not I won't throw the bowl at you. The crockery is safe. If you must stay, then you must. But be aware, the smell may offend, the light and sound may grate on the nerves. And amid all this horror there is a purity and the purity burns. It is like acid. Like distilled battery acid. And this is the purity I have waited a life for. This is why I am. The Papacy is in turmoil, the monarchy is in tatters, the butchery is in full flavour, in full swing. But the pure is becoming more distilled. I am in a thought, in a manner of thinking. And that is that I am trying to put myself on a sort of gallows with this writing. With this constructivism. But once more I am the bungler, the inept, the fool. For the gallows I build are for the child. The hangman's noose would not fit my big toe. This is not planned. It is in the manner of the outcast who is doomed to be presented with the ridicule of this exile. On the border of the desert I am writing about a thousand thousand comedians who do naught but crack jokes and sift the slime. As it is I do not know privacy. The people I walk past in the street have seen me as beggar, as thief, as fool, as pretence. I have left a trail of these things like a sinking elephant. Indeed, I have blown my trumpet the entire trip. In some sort of celebration. Some sort of Candice. The purity I feel is the burning in the guts which one cannot mistake. It is the funeral pyre you are shown but cannot have. It is already occupied. You wake from a dream to find it out in the street in full view and you find yourself burning already in it. You wish to chant. To sit and watch the brains bubble and the juices splutter. And you know that it is real. You know something has begun, has passed out of the mind and into eternity. It is the freedom of the illusionaire. Of the illumiere. I am sitting in the park. At night. The city is close around me and I am in discomfort. The harlequin comes and sits beside me, silent. There is a lesson, in that all is the confusion of the non-lesson. The silent, mystical parable. The harlequin begins to pull feathers out of his head and I choke. I know not why. It is as if I am being disembowelled from the head downwards. I look for barbed wire to rub my throat against, but precautions have already been taken. We are in an age when all is known, yet I think that the many stray atoms of the human beings that wander with madness and the sacred surge of an intent not even calculated will have an impact on those that pretend to the accomplishment, the perfection. The only perfect shape I have been able to find in the city all day is that of a dog turd. And that was on the footpath of the Police building. In the night the cry comes to me like that of the musselman. And it is singular and it is splendid. Whether of the human or the animal or the demon I know not but it contains the spirit of the earth. And as such is sacred. I am for the singular. I am for the repertoire that is chaste and sacred. I am for the meaning which still has mystery. I am for the 'DOG'. Give us our bread with a little bit of the undefined on it please. Give us something without all the answers already ticked. I adeptly tucked away the sound in my mind. I replay it. I return outside and myself howl at the moon. I whisper to imaginary people, imaginary loves. Such has my life come to. Most of the love I practice these days, I do not practise, I commit. I wield the phallus through the air and it is pink and electric. It is black magic. The great night clouds dance. The moon hums. The elements unite. Gone is the scattered order and in its place the wholeness of the rite. Of the Ideal. I take a rock and after painting it pink and black in the manner of one of Guillaume's drawings pray to it. It is the Idol. And I know not what even prayers I give issue to. The process is enough. I am adoring the life in myself. I am praying to the human race to the esprit.

But the disenchantment, the distaste is not so readily dispelled. After several weeks I am disgusted. The human race invites such. Next I am praying to the human heart. So that men might know men. So that the hollow but poisonous walls might be brought down. The idol cannot bear the flame and splits. I throw it away. Into the garbage. And throughout the night strange chants fill the air and the night seems to shudder black on black. When it feels that I have written enough of myself, when the description is replete, again the magic borders begin to merge, begin to depopulate and I must continue. Do not mistake me, I mean to finish. I will not deliver a half-baked vegetable to your plate. I mean to write to you a true account that may give you indigestion, heartburn and flatulence but nevertheless one you can get your teeth into. I am making love to a woman. The night has been going well. There has been dining and romance but the instant there comes for the climax an indescribable urge comes upon me to strangle her fine neck. She inquires of my thoughts as if in a telepathy and I stumble around the room as if in an overdosed state. The compliment of truth only acquires the ridicule, only receives the suspicion. So I am silent. So I maintain a mystery that is melting and soiling the carpet. So I am transfixed. The gift is all package. And the true present has been broken and thrown away eons ago. I am looking through my friend's collection of weird letters to the media. He is an internee in a Bedlam. He speaks of mayhem, of murder and violence and manslaughter but his biggest bugbear is that his ears run. It seems the liquid ear-wax would fill milk bottles. He is wondering if it might qualify him for some sort of employment. Perhaps as a circus oddity. I am at a loss. There can be no answer for some intimacies. He is writing around to all the media shows about these and other related experiences.

All this appeals to me. To my finer sensibilities. It's like watching snails and slugs cavorting in shit. It has the other side to it also. In the moonlight the shit is just a shadow or a silhouette, and the snail's trails are a magic silk. He is like a surrealist gone truly mad. Gone truly creative. Please, give me the more merrier metaphor. Something with a bit of dirt and dung and fecundity about it. Spare me the reference to fine breath and silk flowers. I can no more than bring myself to accept the fine palaver of sweet smells and bovine eyes, than I can fly over the moon. I will not have such things in my life. They perpetuate the lie. Over and over again the songs and stories and poems whine in their educated, over-accentuated accents and it is like living in a fresh rain to find the crude image such as the sculptor or the artist of life would make. Give me the bizarre, the flawed, the blemished and the tainted image. Only then does it smack of authenticity and realness and compassion. I read of piles of skulls being found in the form of pyramids in Asian countries after bouts of slaughter. Surely this image of horror does more for us than to read of pretty flowers and fragrant odours. Put a little dirt in my images please so they won't decay in my mind. So that they will foster something, so that I will feel something; give life and not boredom. I am from out-side. It is night. The moon looks like a great female form; a great egg. But the egg is teeming with all manner of life. Only could it have such a contemplation, such a manner of the aloof as it has. And the great female of it looks as if it is bursting to piss and will do so on the oneiric clouds that surround, such is the sublime look upon it. On nights such as these the scream in myself becomes a little quieter a little more playful and is like to make musical sounds and play up and down the scales a bit. I recall times which have nowhere else to go. I remember parts and members of memories which are the left-over pieces of the game. I am in the public toilets at the city train station. People are coming and going in a flurry of liquid sounds and the slamming of doors. The atmosphere already pleasant to begin with as you can see is made strange by the roaring overhead of trains. It is rush hour and the trains are coming and going like metal monsters. It is as if a constant chanting is occurring. I feel as if I am inside the primordial atom that exploded to make the universe. Such is the import of the chaos and confusion. There are voices but also the strange silences of men going about the business of pissing and defecation. The chants get louder and louder. The man in the cubicle next to mine is praying to his god. It is the cavern of the mad asshole and the monks are praying for early rain. Such is the nature of the whimsy of human nature for itself. Outside a woman is screaming and no-one is game to go out. The stars are out tonight also and flicker like a psychotic's eyes. If pressed, I will say that they splutter in their serenity like the sparks that are made when you piss on a fire. Like the sparks that make themselves when a live-wire cable is driven thru the cranium of a lunatic. I am blessed by the image and cursed by the reality the image brings. The explosion is a delight but the torn flesh from the projectiles something to reckon with. But on we go nevertheless, dear reader. We will get there. To the finish. Or better still, to a finish. I must commend anyone who is still with me through this assortment of words. Let me say it is no easier for me than it is for you. I am in pain also, let me assure you. Again images come to my mind. Now that I have started the process with the bloody moon and stars there comes a flood. A deluge. I am whispering to myself in front of a typewriter in a lighted kitchen. It is the early hours of the morning. It is like I am surrounded by cadavers in perfect condition. Occasionally air bubbles escape and one of these corpses makes a sound. Only when you carefully approach do you find out that the world is not dead but simply passed out, simply in slumber. They are going to rejuvenate in a few hours time and then again all sorts of mayhem will begin. All manner of the atrocity will begin over again. All about me is the nebula. And it is in a fury. It is raining to earth tiny green frogs, nails, tongues, intestines, mayhem. It is my personal storm. But I have no control over it. Quite the reverse, it dominates and directs my life. In it people vaporise, disappear, everything is swept into it. It is making me an Outsider, more and more with each of its incredulous rains. First the spot, the heebie-jeebies, then the black plagues of the soul. I am in torment but have long since realized that I am in love with my unknown torturer. I am craving his brutal hands, his clenched teeth and the obscenities that his mouth brings forth. Under his hands I am like a young woman. This is my God. The recurrent psychosis, the spitting wheel of knowledge, the burnt out eyes that have destroyed beauty to accomplish knowledge. I have plucked and eaten the apple and survived, but have been puking in the corner ever since the first bite. All around me are the voices and I am told by those in the know that they are forbidden. That they are a delusion, that they don't exist. But I know better. The voices are in every aspect of the furious, of the truculent and pure of the tender and of the intimate. I did not invite them to me. The divine rained them upon me whilst I was making prayer and sacrifice. I have taken myself to the chopping block and have been slaughtered. The remains have returned to the storm and made the pretence of life. I look upon those around me and see the incredible. The glue that keeps all their parts together still continues its function. The grease that they eat to oil their gears is still functioning. The lubrications they apply to their organs are still working. I am in dread of this army around me, the populace. For they are pulling in every direction. They are so totally sane that they have superseded the clinically insane. In a state of catatonia each single entity stares into a full-length mirror and caresses himself, herself. And the caressing is hopeless and helpless. They are just wearing each other away. Each touch brings the destruction of the Temple, brings the dead of the cells. But this is the modern urban. This is the city and the Delusion by which these people sleep peacefully; or delude themselves into thinking that they do. I would like to write dear reader with the intent to do some damage. I would like to stir up the muds for along with the blindness comes the initiation and the holocaust. These gods do not leave footprints they leave stark visions and a hand composed of fingers of fire. I am alight. I am burning but I do not combust. I do not waste, I am not consumed. But enough. I rave about the gods, I am uncertain to whom I communicate. Whom I adore. I possess a monomania, but it's the voice in my ears of the angels, of the seraphim, of the sweetbread of discovery and life. The problem in this symphony of words is that there comes crescendo after crescendo and one is stumped what to write next. Every time the instruments go crashing off stage and the curtain falls one is enervated to the point of hysteria. The difficulty is in maintaining the trance, to pick up the fallen body of expression off the street, to drag it out of bed, to kick a bit of energy into the enervation.

In this music the thread is constantly coming out of the needle and one is tempted to pack together the whole baggage and cast it overboard. But at the last moment before destruction a new idea blurts along and wants to be included, so I continue. It is after all, the notes of a demented. I am sick, now, of being in the desert, I want to go to a holiday resort. To lay in the sun and fuck beautiful women. But stuff you, you crazy schizo, avant, avant, forward, on with the danse d'boire on with this menagerie of words. More vowels, equality for consonants, hang this excuse for the English language up and continue. We have attractions from the Pit which will shock, which will entice, which will make you sit bolt upright in your beds, which will make you swoon in god knows what mood.

I am thinking of some of the more grandiose hallucinations and manias that have occurred to me over the past ten years. There have been times when I have felt myself to be approaching the very source. To be crossing a border that I have been searching for for years. I am involved with 'EYE'. This is an occasion of the pure phantasmagorical. These are extra-terrestrials all with the drives of life but arse-up. They are cock-sure but their equation is incomplete, is not the full quid. I have been racing through space with them: after having converted the city to outer space and we are merrily blowing planets to the shit-house in a mad helter skelter effort to create everything and anything. I am inside a nightclub and am pounding the bar so forcefully that I am leaving knuckle prints in it. Eye is swarming about the planets like every being on earth gone psychotic and the music has the finesse of drain cleaner and the sweat is pouring off the very walls. In this position I stay for hours. Until the mania is at last settled. If I am not bounced I will quietly wipe the moisture off my psychosis and polish it a little and alight to some other setting. That is what is misunderstood. The act of madness is infinitely flexible, is a living growth, and can be made to pertain to all situations. Beta Ordovician Eye, the little devil, snuck into my masterbatorium but instead of pressing the button to start the masturbation machine mistakenly pressed the destruct button and the whole space fleet went up like a giant mushroom farting itself into non-existence. Such is the fragility of the mania. The wolf is at my door. But then so is the lion, the gorilla, the ox, the hyena, the cobra, Piltdown Man, the tsetse fly and the hoax. There is no situation that I can think of that has not occurred in my lifetime. I have been murdered and floated down the muddy river. I have been mugged and waited in the gutter for salvation and eternity. My perversions fill notebooks and march down the street every Sunday with the Salvation Army band. I move. It is enough. It is the divinity. This is that which is infinite. This is what I interpret to be. Glory to the moments. Glory to the finesse of a woman's arm and the great dam of passions that such a thing will cause to erupt. Glory be to the beggar in the street and his continuum. Glory to the confusion, and the myriad. In all this I have had an overdose. I am accursed. I am not only a psychotic, but a recurrent psychotic. I am plugged into the Machine, but it is I who control it not vice versa as should be. While the doctors are so casually and seriously-minded looking at the scopes and gauges I can make the electronic utterances mimic the most profound and elongated farts. And all this without a smile on my face. All this in the most likewise serious manner. I am respected because I am a good subject. Stick out your tongue please and I stick out my tongue. Sit upright please and I sit upright. Cross your legs please and my legs are already crossed. But still the farts whine all about the room to the tune of Oh, Susanna, or sometimes, "Give me all of your lovin". I am fresh from a nightmare and it seems that it has been going on forever. The situation is made all the more in that I have had my eyes open for its entire duration. As I say, I am fresh from a dream and it has left my body stinging with the tincture of burning sulphur, with the scent of carbolic acid, with the stench of faeces and of rotten meat. And lost within this dream was all that was I. I begin to think. I begin to look around myself at the other inhabitants of this planet. I find them as fragile in their hopes and pretences and joys as myself. I weep for them. That the slightest fracture will cause the egg to burst. That the slightest tremor will cause the cup to spill the contents so laboriously prayed to, awaited for, made into thus. Amid all the paradises that you and I can manufacture in a lifetime lies the rapine and the asunder. The flowers sink in the mud; the songs choke in the distance. Even the dream which materialises which seems to maintain itself will someday go mad with a meat cleaver in one hand, the carving knife in the other. So there is thought to Sisyphus. But this creation does not do justice. I would rather think that we will manage to climb the devastating mount, but, arriving exhausted and expired at its summit collapse, dead into some pit of anti-climax. And if we (or the unlucky ones) escape this fate then there awaits the diabolical and calculated slaughter of a mind that we have created but deny is ours. It is no wonder that the wondrous that overtakes the human race is always of the most diabolical and censorious nature. We stare at the great flames that erupt from the furnace and stand dumb, but the fuel is the life of our souls, the image with us since we began. So it is that we should see the sham that is our manufacture and not the dust. Would that it was dear reader, a composition so inert and without deceitful connotation. But in amongst this great aureole of the cursed lie the delights, like Hottentots on a rampage. Like drunk and paralytic faeries. Like beasts with their legs amputated. We have no response other than to confront them and make pleasure from them. A pleasure that will not protect from the sharp piercing of the knives and devices of hell but that will numb and give solace in the off days. The days when our captors and torturers, which are actually ourselves, give respite. But why should I become so involved with the human race? What are they to me? I am surprised. I have been speaking in the common plural and this is unusual. Better to stick to the undeniably singular and not suffer the refutation of those that think rotten eggs are petunias. Do you know that I am lunatic? Do you know how many times I have been devastated? And yet borne on the wings of the delusion that is catastrophic is manna. Is the bread of existence. Think of it. To be deluded. To be without light. The things that I have seen in this darkness you would not believe. It is as if the very soul of creation unabashed now that the lights were off casually stripped to the skin in my presence. And the distortions and imaginings that go in hand with the darknesses are profound. I have made love to visions, to forms that have held a beauty as if the physical that would take your breath away and when I have touched the soft skin of a breast or a vagina, moths have erupted from the mouth, from the anus, from the nostrils, from the cunt itself and in their swarming have made patterns and designs of rapturous beauty. I have been buried alive under these moths in nights when it seems that each hard star in the sky is the very spark of existence. I have touched the hollow in myself where amid the monstrous also lies the divine. Amid the putrescent ganglia there have been sparks of fire, real fire that has blistered into raging storms of flame, that has penetrated to the innermost and burnt asunder all the confusion of a life filled with mayhem and distraction.

In the bowels of the filthiest concoction angels have arisen singing and in the witness is the divine for it is not beyond you to realise that this performance (call it what you will), is for you alone, singularly.

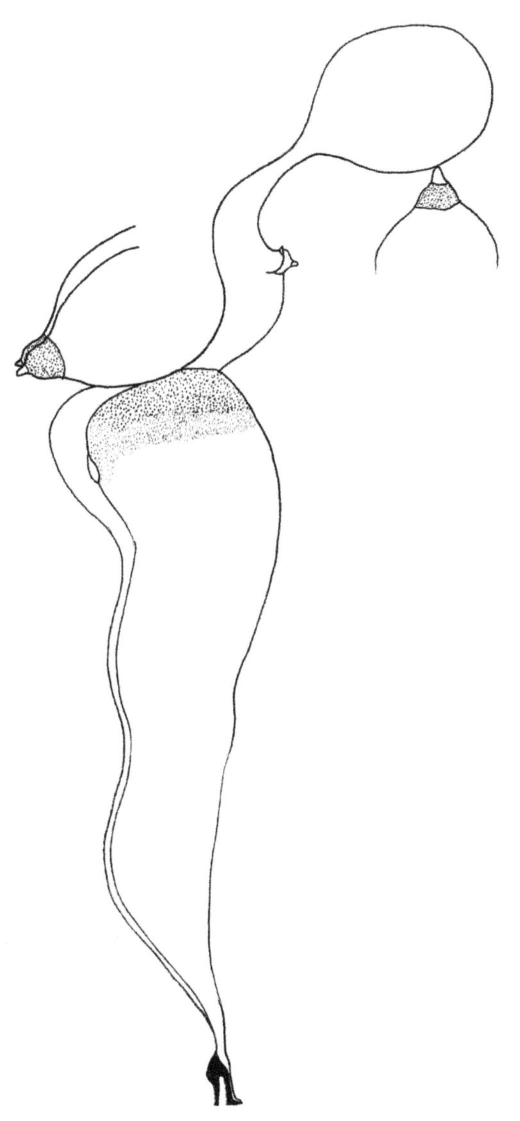

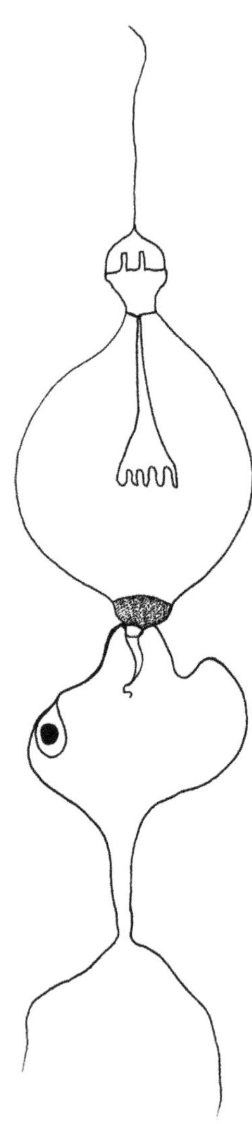

The Light Bulb Eaters

I suppose that there is some value in keeping the blinkers on, in treading the straight and narrow, in following the letter of the bible and giving them a quick polish while you're at it and NOT selling your soul, but then when your card comes up, it's only worth a few miserable nickels and most of it gets thrown away, uneaten as with an exotic, over-ripe cheese that you buy when you are being extravagant …

20.5.93
Sydney

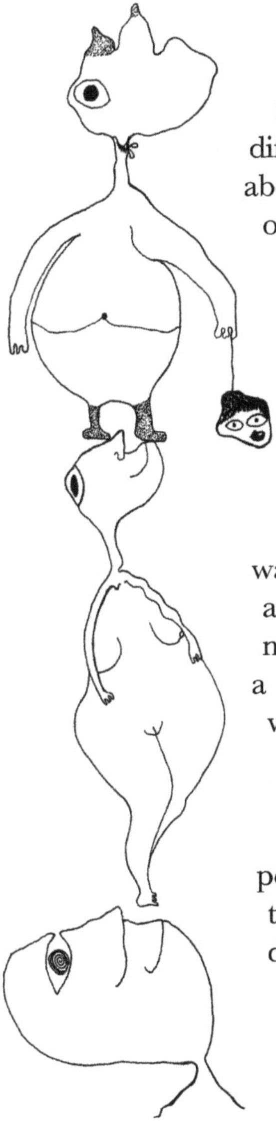

The prolonged study of chaos is behind me 1989, 1990, 1991 and 1992 were difficult years indeed. This study brought about a psychic topography which was one of extremes. I cannot quite come to an apt description of what its experience is like, even now. If asked, I would have to say that it is truly Charon the Boatman excepting the river is hideous and blinding and the boat beyond any sense or logic. In my work I seemed to use only the absence of colour – black, and then it was used in wild, recondite ways that tore at the heart but liberated the spirit. For months I could see under the floor boards a vast, gnashing black cavernous mouth which issued forth an unbelievable stink as decayed molars oozed voluminous pus from the abscessed remains of their roots while the mouth gnashed like the percussion section of a symphony orchestra playing at twice the tempo and blind drunk.

Strangely enough I was eminently serene during this manifestation; I saw nothing more than the disorder in life trying to eat through the floorboards. Anyway, I had a point fixed before my eyes as if it was welded to the air. What concerned me was power and its acquisition. I had an obsession with regard to this. What I could see were places. Unscaleable, impenetrable places that contained what I wanted and I wished issue. Luckily the orthodontic magic shop-prop went away, but then this was replaced by ever more horrible, ever more bewildering apparitions, so much so that I could give them no names and my serenity was dismissed.

A new thing infested the house – it was the ghost of a woman that could become solid and I was driven insane by the smell of her. With her advent I became as if espoused of this state, chaos. That is not to say that my life was a tribulation but one night found me sitting by the grey steel and escape of the railway wanting to find a way to ordinariness. The reverse became into play, I was taken further towards the core in a locomotive that could not exist even in one's wildest dreams, driven by a one-eyed monomaniac accelerating faster and faster towards a destination that could bear no life.

A trip to hell would have been preferable but by the time I was this discriminating there was not the slightest iota of control, nor could be.

It was on this helter-skelter that a plethora of visions occurred. They themselves represented another order of life … it was the realm of the irrational. Here I found myself. It was that I became a star performer on par with any in this florid over-grown miasma of the picturesque and ceaseless change. Anything was possible, the troupe of personalities and entities was endless and I changed as rapidly as the place. It became obvious to me that here the real stuff of life permeated and I would journey from vision to vision with an ease that was never mine in the concentration logic of the Western

World. Things came from everywhere. There was no such thing as the source, or the beginning, rather anything had a right to be from the most profound to the most irrelevant, and came from anywhere.

It was here that I understood the voice of things. Amid a fertility of the visual everything had its utterance. This is the true dream where everything is imbued with its own life and independent raison d'être and definition and its classification unknown and unwanted.

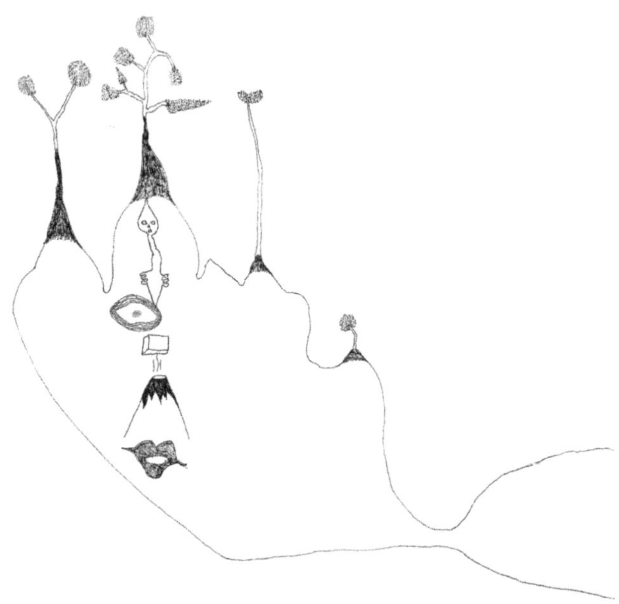

But to return to chaos. I could not contend with theoreticians who were deluding themselves that they could fit the idea into their file cabinets. I had absolutely no interest in talking to them. A journey is not a piece of paper with mathematical derivations on it no matter how one might look at it, and I regarded this armchair complexity as sham.

I found that when one enters into an arrangement with chaos one becomes on a singular stance with violence. The delight was that all connation would be absent. I found myself lost in a place of inestimable power and unbroached beauty. It was that as a being you could approach an abstract force. Yet this was only the outskirts of the body and it attracted all.

It was a later time that took me to the core of the realm of psychosis. Given such a bedlam of walls and their intricacies, this place is a city that can never be mapped, where today's freeway is tomorrow's impasse, where familiar landmarks are gone in an instant like beasts burning in the field whilst standing up, where a Houdini-like power is needed simply to go from step to step, where to imagine is the deadliest of all arts for you bring that into being, and it has an untamed life of its own, where one day everything is inanimate and the next animate, where in dismantling one wall one creates many more, where one might be accosted by a thug and one can be in no way sure that it is not a product of the mind or something from another dimension, where everything overwhelms to such a crescendo that one could be in the middle of the Atlantic during a pitched storm and sitting on a piece of board.

Yet this is only a town in a place where yet there is the wild country. The term of explanation for this place is bitter, for one can only see where one has been; hindsight where there is no order or logic indicates nothing of what is ahead and indeed contrives hazards which because they do not obey any logic, defy solution.

My exploration of such towns and cities was seventeen years long. I found the entry as difficult as the exit. As a child I would often sit and entrance myself upon the visual trying to find a door. It was as much because I was assured that an incomparable joy lay within as to escape the emotional barrage of family which was already attempting to tailor me for a useless pedestrian life. Later, the delights of mania became accessible after a concerted effort at sleep deprivation. This was a place where one could be da Vinci for a night. In a fit one could eat up ideas as at a banquet, and in the prolonged, elongated, disembowelled, distended organs of the night create wonders of the imagination. At times it felt that the entire five hundred geniuses of Greece were all working in unison as in a liverwurst factory where the conveyer belt was greatly speeded up.

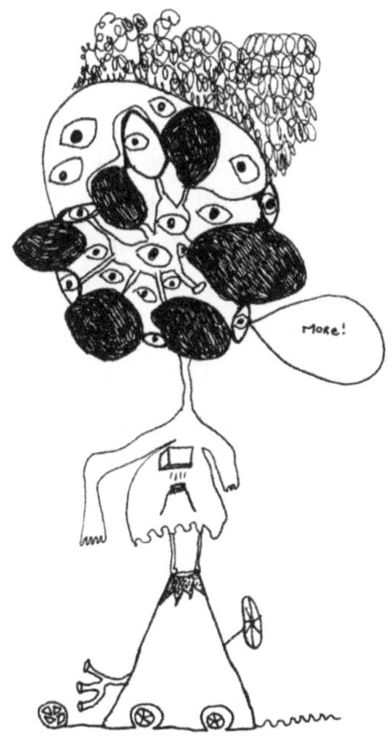

What was created would have to be judged also by the obscene come-down of the morning and as in the poem Howl by Ginsberg, one would be the owner of handfuls of gibberish and not really sure what to do with them. But the essence of these nights, years of them, was flight and it was as a young Icarus that I could see everything of my suburban neighbourhood, and went higher. I awoke; the sky had that steely grey colour mixed with its blue to indicate that it was afternoon. The next I noticed anything with what we term consciousness, it was apparent that it was the early hours of the morning. I could tell from the traffic. For a dozen hours everything had been flattened by a narcotic wind bringing d'oubli, who was I now after this?

What movie theatre had I fallen asleep in and then what was a moist usherette doing on my lap oh! with her pussy spread like an angel about to fly? Surmises, guesses, speculations – here for the first time these were not my enemy and I entranced duality as a state of existence.

I came to a place that should have been the epitome of horrors. It was a closely contained room that paradoxically held endless shelving. On these shelves were every description of head that had been removed from a torso. Each was still living, by some concoction of magic and collectively every manner of base emotion, vice and mood was represented. In this place was a low light, the type used for interrogations and amid these heads, and endless ruminations, murmurs, screams, historical narratives. I found the place akin to musical composition and terrorless and with the hidden things I gained access to, began to build a contraption within myself which I named the toy of the spirit. Its purpose was coherent, which was unusual for me for I had been at will with the irrational for two decades to remove the cloying things of the world from my life.

Meanwhile, I had an enigmatic and esoteric study. I regard paradox as both a state of being and a place rather than the conventional systemization. This place was my workshop where I could turn the ugly things I had acquired into the opposite. I matched this with the making of small sculptures, so that parts came into my possession. I was also dismantling this realm of paradox, I considered it in no way sacrosanct which would then somehow translate into solid objects.

I had an illusion. I was in a strange field. I had landed there in a flying device which I dismantled and reassembled into a motor car and I toured this wondrous brazen field which became yet more wonderful because its brazenness never ceased. What is more I knew, for fact it never would. The delicious dance was like blond light fibres undulating in an icy electrified sea, their dance delicately touching every nerve-ending and the sheer amass of water that made them move quietened me.

I returned to where I had landed and found two sets of wings carefully folded into bundles. One of the bundles was mine – I had never realized that I had wings. There was a storm like mirrors breaking but that was alright for it made the place rampant. It wasn't at all that I became discontent with this place, rather the mischief I have, took hold of me once more and I decided to journey. I drove to the edge and proceeded down the pale-cool alabaster brow. Often I would stop the motor and alight and give small kisses to this surface and then re-embark and proceed on my way. I know what she was feeling; she must have imagined she was being beset by tiny moths. After a while I became greatly excited and looming on the horizon were the twin peaks of her breasts like two meteorites of silky soapstone that had struck the earth and became ways it could talk. I began to accelerate; and I could no longer speak. Although I sang bawdy songs in a quiet manner, when I was sure no-one was about.

The journey seemed to take on another scope … where there are no walls, no barriers, there are no reflections, no necessities. I arrived at last. They were splendid. It was in a trance that I stayed here. I forgot where I had parked my motor. Through a lascivious gorge narcotic zephyrs came giving me visions of immense, outlandish, disobedient flowers and a sense of bareness I had never known. I did dark dances about the nipples until everything became odorous and sweaty and great stupa loomed in the air like those of the Borobudur.

Lost in an unclad paradise so sharp as to incite acute madness I gained access to the fires of the desert prophets. I was struck with visions of the lower, darker realms; I grabbed my hat and found my motor and proceeded towards a blond but primeval jungle of dreams and delirium that I could see constantly beckoning before my eyes. I travelled across a great plain which was unaccountably luxurious; so much so that it was only with a profound force of will that I didn't alight from my motor and sink into this fabric, for I knew I would fall asleep with the great pounding that was its planet forever. This place was luminous, composed out of the fibre of the moon and in its midst was a circular chasm from whence I could hear talk of every type of life.

I was beginning to be in a hurry now, and yet at the same time a state of intoxication was coming upon me. It was as if I was in bondage with my destination and held there by the tentacles of an octopus covered with fur. On the horizon arose a vast mound covered by a salty-coloured ginger fur. Within pulsed antiquities of the blood, bloods from other places, bloods from other beings. I stopped the motor and took my shoes off and entered the forest and from the first step was electrified. Overhead the most awesome of skies moved. Within its emotions were intricacies of total illogic so that one became mesmerised, seduced, awakened. The sky was tart green. When I put my ear to the floor of the forest, strange things arose, moths that looked like bats only they were multi-coloured, miniature pink flamingos that burst into flames, butterflies with the heads of cats, small white lilies and magenta lotus that were multi-legged and jumped like outrageous grasshoppers, insects bearing many heads with perfectly formed smooth legs covered by sheer nylons, centipedes and millipedes that bore miniature combat helmets and carried tiny machine-guns and scooted off to the trenches, strange plump berries that had faces on them and were squeezed tight with drunken hallucinogens.

From unknown places came the somnambulistic voice of a woman moaning in her sleep with things unfathomable. My sense of time did not operate in this forest and I do not know how long I wandered in the light from the penumbra between insanity and absolute lucidity. When hungry I ate honey that came from the fur. I wandered without direction and needing none. Nevertheless, I grew fervent with intent and started ploughing forth to a great edifice that already possessed me. My arrogance was cut short but not my obsession, I became engrossed in a copse of wet moving fur the colour of fox that bound me to it. No matter with what strength or determination I expressed, I was held affixed to the bone-warm pulse and flesh – there was sometimes a woman's soft laughter which seemed to have no floor. It was not I that went to this place, but that it came to me and with a body of so much darkness that all previous paths became asphyxiante.

I hear another woman moan. It's unearthly how such things can be heard years later. She had the ability to turn one into a woman with all a woman's internal finery with a magical power she hardly understood. Two scorpions, we became joined at the genitals and all division ceased. While we did this ritualistic dance we imbibed drunken fluids made from carnivorous plants and the genitals and glands of animals and secret places. We seemed never to leave the house, never to talk; the only thing I remember besides her is the bed.

All that water that we held between us by our zodiac could not contend with any containing and a confusion started that took the last dregs of the intellectual from us and firmly buried our bodies in the primeval erotic with a force and concussion that was shattering. Making love on that bed for months amid an enormous herd of cattle being slaughtered by a pick-axe through the cranium and waiting to be slaughtered brought about a physiological change whereby we became awash constantly with enormous volumes of adrenalin, and to be able to co-habit with the sheer hysteria of the herd.

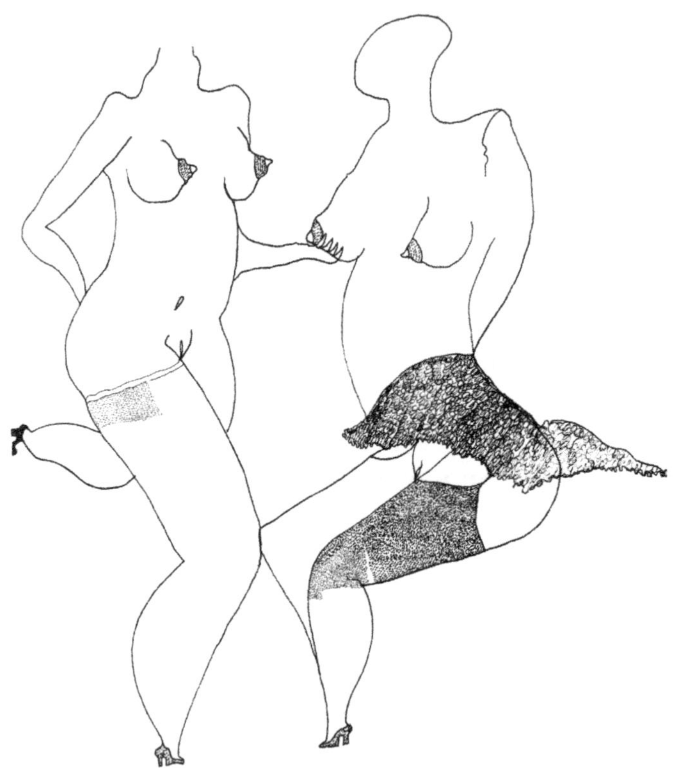

Endomorphs, orgasms became blackly terrible and held an unsurpassed addiction. The house contained many more things than it should have. When I listen I hear screams of lovers tortured by pleasure in one of the hells of Dante and the woman beside me moaning in her sleep.

The aftermath was six months in a place I called the engine-room. Here, in the bowels of a grey metal ship of gargantuan proportions steaming from pole to pole I was jarred and vibrated by a mechanical, crystalline ferocity intent upon destroying everything about me.

The visionary took on an acrid sharp-edged horror and harassment from which there was no escape. It was as if I was a piece of machinery occupied by far too many revs that threatened to be shaken to bits. What's more, to make concrete the analogy, I found myself locked in a dim, miniscule, dirty grey-white room in the local bedlam.

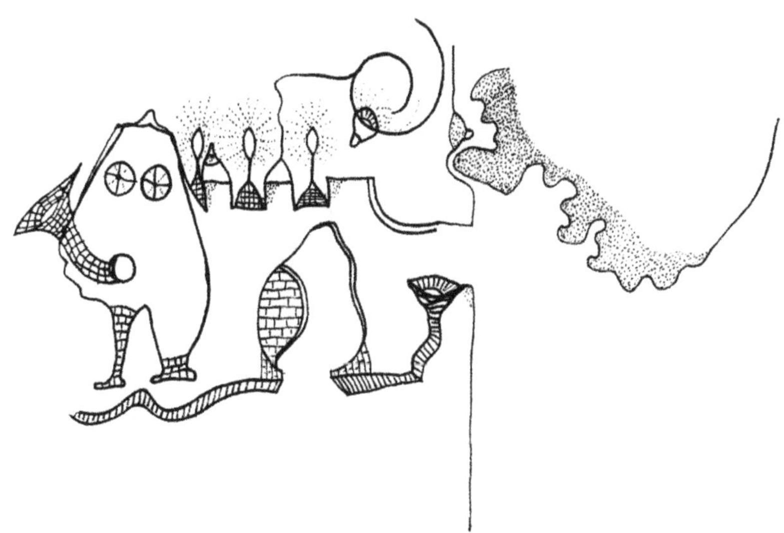

The madhouse proved an eventful place amid the unrelenting boredom that it typifies and produces as currency to dole out in useless amounts to its inmates.

Every known form of freak and mutation inhabit there and this includes the staff. The enormity belied by the ordered plantation of beds and manicured lawns is incurable, ungraspable and of an order to shock anyone from their senses, lunatic or otherwise.

It produces a place of numbness deep in the brain which itches like it is being beset by a field of fleas but cannot be scratched and a further feeling of a ferret burrowing into the remnants of one's umbilical cord.

It is why people are having constant fights.

Why people are throwing and smashing crockery

Why people are drowning themselves face down in the water-gardens.

Why people are gnawing at raw stones.

Why Peter Linford has to be dragged up the stairs by his heels … his head plonk! plonk! plonk, like a pendulum clock with its neck broken.

Why the birds fly backwards and upside down across the joint and fall from the air without logic, why the lunatics beat their heads against walls precisely at the solstice, why nothing seems to work except in reverse.

They serve it to you in your morning flat, cold tea. For those disillusioned with the chaotic-minded, and anything else, it is the place to be.

AUTHENTICITY

Every evening on his way back to Ward 25 Tony passes the Temple of the Dog; & the Dog, knowing that Tony is an authentic inhabitant of this city within a city, lets him pass unmolested. Tonight, however, when Tony approaches the Temple, the dog begins to howl as though to question Tony's authenticity. As far as Tony is concerned this questioning is totally uncalled for, & in protest he picks up a stone & hurls it at the Dog. But the howling continues; in fact, it has grown considerably louder. Another stone, & the howling is joined by that of another dog. Several more stones, not one of them finding its mark, & the whole neighbourhood is in an uproar. And now there are no more stones in the area, so Tony must go down to the river to find more. He fills his rucksack &, straining under the weight, returns to the Temple. A hairline crack has appeared in Tony's authenticity. It now has the potential to crack into two pieces like an old saucer. If this miserable excuse for a dog isn't silenced, Tony's done for. He's much too brittle to be mended. But perseverance finally pays off; the last stone in the rucksack hits the Dog, & the Dog, again satisfied with the authenticity of the devotee who has rendered this homage, allows Tony to pass. But by now it's very late, & Tony's absence has been noticed. When he gets back to the Ward he will be told that his Category C privileges have been revoked.

Phillip Hammial – Sydney
January 13, 1988

People are incorrect when they consider lunatics to be aimless. For each there are the set destinations, the places to visit and explore, the re-routings, the detours and the embankments, the final destination. Across a lawn-grass runs a lunatic in pyjamas, he sees the promised land and is out after it for all he's worth. On his heels is a nurse with a syringe. The closer he gets to seventh heaven, the faster she runs.

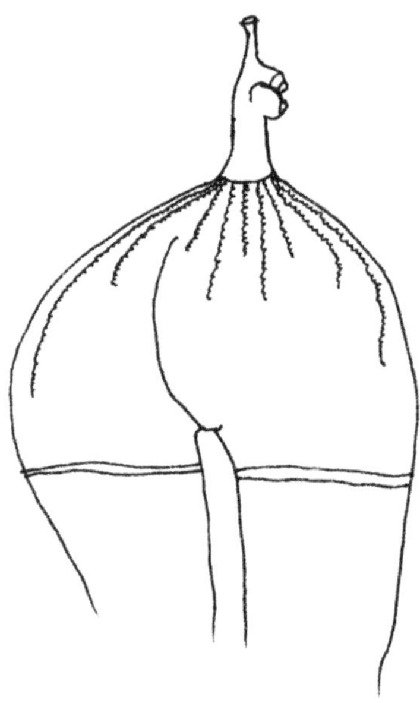

Near the frog-pond she crash-tackles him about the legs being absolutely sure to hang on to the syringe. She is wearing glass stockings held up by a lacy black garter-belt with red trim … her dress has become hiked up above her waist in the foray… buttons are missing from her blouse and one breast is leering … the lunatic is petting this with one hand while his mouth is buried on her cunt … he is biting off mouthfuls of her black lace panties and swallowing them.

She is repeatedly jabbing him in the buttocks with the point of the syringe and spurting oily liquid over both of them … very little of the substance seems to be finding its way into the lunatic. Eventually both collapse unconscious from sheer exertion … in the sunlight one can see the dispersion of light in the drop of tranquiliser which has become affixed to the very tip of the nurse's nose like a gob of snot.

Perhaps, when exploring the psychotic, if one had a wish to use, one would wish for a navigation device, some form of compass to indicate the direction of things. But none, no matter how ingenious, would work. The nearest one can get is art. Where the art of the mannered moderns and contemporaries has failed to penetrate this place is that they never cared to enter it, being content or discontent to prowl the outer perimeters scavenging remnants and bits of half-eaten carcass and calling them found objects of the subconscious or unconscious. It was unquestionable that a generation would happen of those who had paid their dues in psychosis, madnesses, explorations and pointless but successful rebellions, of those that felt comfortable, adjusted and worthwhile in unordinary, alien or altered states.

By 'alien' I don't mean alienated or outcast, I mean that lucidity and way of seeing where there is no mundane.

Being at an exhibition of this art brut gives a way to see the unordinary state as if into a partly faceted diamond. Here outlandish beasts walk along a mountain path on a walking mountain singing, the mountain you discover, much to your delight is singing also; furthermore you are taken into infinity when you finally discover the beasts are walking backwards down the spiral path to the legs of the mountain and down them. To top it off, you look to the apex of the mountain and there is your host waving greetings to you.

What we have here is an art which is also a poetry and a travelogue of places that are entirely unlisted at the local travel agent. This habitation in the wilder poetical places of the mind is an ancient art in itself. When one looks at the cave paintings of Lascaux, reads the epic of Gilgamesh, considers the initiations of the Egyptians or looks at the Old Testament, one is given access to an almost unending procession of recalcitrant and self-possessed lunatics bent on only one purpose and that the exploring of the inner sanctum.

Art brut and what it showed of individual's internal cosmology made known that lunatics are not a homogeneous group in toil, that in fact there is the wildest of individual variations to a degree that is not comprehensible. The wide appeal to viewing audiences who say they connect directly with the work leads us to understand that we cannot point in any one place at the lunatic, and if we do we are invariably pointing at ourselves.

Madness is liberation of the soul. It seems to be the Old Testament zealots who were fundamentally and innately aware of this. A large bus pulls up beside a large sandstone rock that is banded with red feldspar. The bands look like fiery snakes, one within another within another devouring themselves. From a distance the stone looks like a brain. The bus stands motionless in the sweltering, simmering heat for what seems an age. Finally, the hydraulic doors open and a parade of sweat-covered lunatics emerges two by two, holding hands, so that they won't get lost. They have been instructed to do this by their keepers who emerge last, keeping as far away from them as possible. One by one, the lunatics let go of each other's hands and start to occupy themselves in the desert. They perform every manner of useless task. One is eating small pebbles, but only the ones made of chocolaty-coloured ironstone, another is trying to mount the brain-rock but continually plummeting onto his back in the sand thereby creating a hole, another is taking notes from god with a pencil and notepad that don't exist and is correcting his grammar along the way. Two lunatics are having a discussion, the one bearing absolutely no correlation to what is being said to the other. Finally, they stand and shake hands in agreement.

One lunatic goes to the nurses who have erected a tent and are now sitting in it and asks for a glass of water. Sane, steely eyes look at him and say something. He understands after about thirty seconds and goes elsewhere to look for water although there is none elsewhere. Finally, Peter Linford goes up to the tent to say that he is Peter Linford and he shouldn't be here. He should be home with his mother. More stony silence and decontaminating looks. But Peter Linford is one who cannot input such a message and he continues to assail the tent and its host, continually, hour after hour, until in a fury at having lost their dignity they manhandle and carry him over to the hole that lunatic B has fashioned in the ground by his repeated falling body. There they bury him up to his neck. It is only with the utmost effort that Peter Linford keeps his new-found secret, that he is sitting on a nest of desert ants.

I cannot think of a state of being more imbued with the absolutes of power nor more accessible than that of chaos. I do not mean entropy, this expansion of things into confusion, nor complexity, which when it becomes daunting, I talk of that place which has as its core pure violence. Unerring chaos, chaos that presents itself as what it is, an elemental force capable of anything in any way with landscapes that do what they wish of their own volition. I kept a documentary of my entrance and initial exploration into chaos – everywhere such words as "violence", "inestimable", "undefinable", "awesome", "ungraspable", "unintelligible", "absolute", abounded on the pages with an immediacy that resembled the fiery chariots in the Veda myths. God was visiting and the deeds of men were either put on high or asundered. Chaos was not a place you could impress with your will. It is a place? State? Being? But it also is contributory for those that could devise a way to survive and withstand the enormous forces involved.

I am standing … I am not sure what is underfoot … it appears to be solid, at least it's holding my weight … but it's non-dimensional … it was a rocky path a moment ago … now it is producing an engulfing feeling of terror that is an animal within that cannot contend with its life being supported by dimensionlessness … nevertheless there is not the plummet of falling to death even if I am experiencing its reaction … I am in one of the falling dreams of subconscious youth … yet I am wide awake. I am sure I am … I think so anyway … long ago anything that contained the slightest complacency or certainty vanished … Moons ago … days, months, are as if the frames of an over-exposed film whipping off a spool … There is no-one there and no projectionist, no-one, nothing except the film ripping off the projection machine … I must do something about my bodily fluids … my piss has turned so dark with the dirty, jolting static of adenalgia that it is almost brown … I must decide what to do here … I appear to be falling upwards into the inside of my head with an incomparable violence while dying from the fall … this surely won't turn any lights on … I move, move into something living … I cannot tell what it is … it is not a companion … one has none here … It seems to be moving with me inside of it … how to get born seems to be the problem … how to find out what one is inside another … now it seems to be inside me and it feels no more comfortable … it's inside my cranium now … and I am expected to think … looming up like a wave from a typhoon in the Pacific Ocean and it's screaming with ferocity that can't be heard but is felt utterly in the body … it seems the inanimate is talking with its own individualist screams of birth yet it is impossible to tell what these substances are and there is no individualism contained there in it all … everything is a mass … rotten, flux … a gargantuan vinyl recording that has melted from the greatest machine of the earth and now comes about one like the first and final wave of the deluge.

I have begun to wonder about the union with this chaos. The thing that cannot be is its reality … one of the things that comes from a creature of such proportions and impartial cruelty is an absolute congress, an absolute memory that is part of your body. Yet it also, almost unbelievably has a silken hand, one that can press sense into the slightest part of the body. I felt I had made an abysmal error by pursuing this encounter into journey when the infrastructure of my life fell away to nothing, and again when I looked scar-laden into the mirror of what is, however, the torn flesh and unsightly scars are how the secrets are hidden and what of my life that didn't get up off the floor by itself I realized should have been shot long ago.

I don't know what to say about my pet study of psychosis. Its one aspect of being intangible precludes any grasp upon it. Psychologists and psychiatrists will be writing theory and case studies till the day the world ends trying to tie their little bits of string from a vast reel labelled "logic", around it. What they do present is a different beast which is not psychosis at all, but what they call illness and they visualize in a meagre form something they wish and not what is.

I have often thought of a cosmos of concentric worlds with unbridled passage of what is between them. Central is the beast of psychosis, its core. Rather than being a neurotically orientated individual like the minotaur, the beast has no name, no meaning, indeed, no substance or being, yet proceeding on subjective reports we are told there is a beast – after all we see and experience psychosis from our eyes not the beast's.

At this point a logical mind will interfere but it is the reverse that interests us, the illogical body.

What is psychotic experience other than stored data and the journey ever more than conceivable avenues through the irrational, illogical and intangible?

Nor should the beast be considered only a denizen, to partisan it is logical and in this instance is a miscreation.

If one gathers about the concentric worlds we see their scope – there is infinity about all of them and they are restructuring irrationally, illogically, beyond the scope of the wildest reproducing organisms.

One must make a hole in oneself to be within this place, of some sort, in some way … the logical fabric requires tearing, the rational core requires breaking only then is it that one registers that there is a hole in reality.

Then that this place is its own reality is obvious, that it isn't my reality or your reality or his reality is irrelevant, it can be entered, journeyed upon, exited, exploited, its landscapes transposed through art;

the place is of the same stuff as its inhabitants,

imbued with a hole,

a broken core that is its centre,

and here you have the beast.

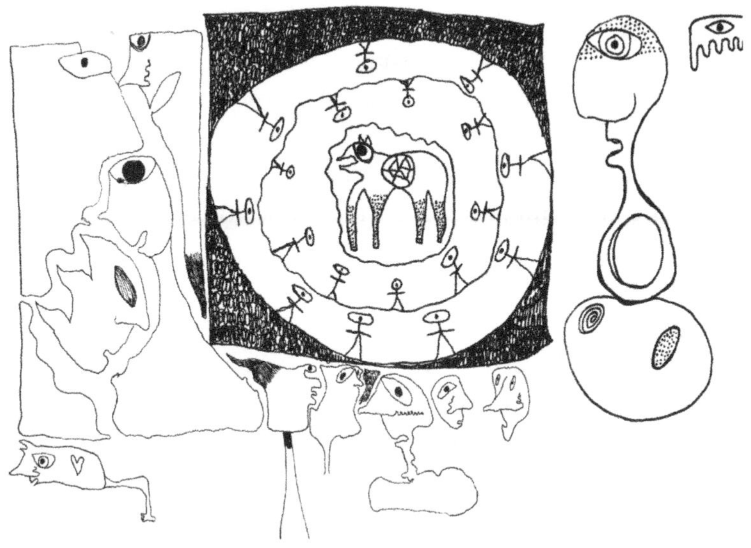

THE BEAST

It appears that there is no entrance or exit to this place, yet I must have gotten in here somehow. My discomfort at the moment is paramount because I cannot remember where I was before I was in here. Perhaps I have always been in here. I cannot conceive of a thunder made out of absolute silence and yet here it is, here I am experiencing it. I cannot tell the dimensions of where I am. There is an alteration like a creature breathing, there is the eternal sound of lungs. I no longer feel the same since being in here. I am in the sea amid a vast swarm of electric tentacles and these have touched everywhere. My life. There was a time when being inside a prison meant nothing to me. It was that I was infinitely capable of finding the sublime and the idyll within. Now I have been touched. It is that I cannot discern the prisons no matter how hard I look.

For a long time I have been uncomfortable with things, with their vacuousness and lack of substance, yet now it occurs to me more and more, and increasingly so that what this is about is the innate feeling of things and not their ostensible apparition which we take as their only reality. Moreso now it feels that I am experiencing a language with things, rather than just looking at their portraits. In this place one can think because there is no logic.

The seventh circle

I've woken up in a furore of bell-ringing, horn-hooting, of animal-bleating, of light-flashing with periodic manner … in a frenzy I am running but there is not the slightest shred of landscape, so I am about nothing with this … then it is recalled that this has been going on unceasingly in my life from the time it began. It's just that I've forgotten it for a second.

In this place I can make not the slightest sense from anything. But nevertheless the place has a piece of humour. In my desperate unease here to put two and two together in any way that makes sense the place is telling me jokes in such a way as to produce on the upside, expressionistic world, a catharsis of frustration and ridiculousness that is mutilating my mind.

My ideas are like an ant's nest at the moment – a labyrinth that is in fact a walking creature composed of creatures. There is no way to schematize this proliferation; before one can even take a breath where one thing is, everything has altered with no relation to anything else or itself. The thing I feel from this place is a burrowing deeper and deeper in my cranium as this creative thought finds still more and more fecund things to plough and devour.

Here in this place one can be deluded into thinking that there is a logic of sorts, at least that there is an order but there is not; what it does do is allow you to project your order, your logic upon it. When that reflection vaporises so does what you were. Only after that does one feel part of what is. One deals with the manifest in a way that this creature-brain you now are is absolutely wanton with antennae and thought becomes continuous explosions and implosions erupting through a tube in the brain as compact substance and colour finally occurs a massive collision as it meets a single heavy atom of flesh located in the darker and older primordial back brain which remains after the human brain and the primate brain have been peeled away and which is of the same substance as the crocodile brain.

The sixth circle

Here I can seem to find every ghost, spectre, apparition and impossible aura with intelligence that is possible. Yet to enter into these things is to risk them walking away with your presence. Yet you are alone except for these entities, and you are compelled to communicate. If anything though, you gather about you the substance that they are composed of. It is a gradual wooing where you become one of them. Of such power is the transfer of identity that you might think yourself another sex or invisible.

It is after a time that you live completely here, the abhorrence and fearsomeness of the terrible visages you come upon cease and you discover that you are conducting business in a coinage of horror, yet you find it acceptable. Nevertheless, if you are sitting on ancient earth where might be inhabiting these beings, you do not sit heavily.

In this world of the sensile and psychic amid the cavernous, enter faces and bodies that could not exist even in the most sensation-seeking sideshow which dispel what they are into feeling about you, one becomes truly heroic. It is how one survives when there is no barrier or shield or weapon that will prevent them. A simple journey into the night involves endless card games with the inhabitants of cemeteries where even the gravestones have crumbled to dust, or conversations with ghostly beings that bear in their appearance every jolting, electric horror about why they are as such or the apparition that will stop the true beat of the heart until its message is deciphered which is always undecipherable until you let it occur upon you. The dictionary one uses in this place is rife – murder, genocide, waste, ravage, suicide, rape, pox, plague, monstrosity, abomination, heinous, horror, cadaverous, hideous … and so forth and so on.

The fifth circle

In this place dream is turned inside out. It is as if looking in, there is a standing of the planet on its axis and then one is inside looking out. All things about you and the world remain the same, it is just that you are inside a fragrant dream from the subconscious. This changes things, it is the very instep of great magicianship – it is possible to dream into the experience what you will, albeit the force of this dream reality is so potent it seems impossible even to lift the smallest stone even with your 'real' hand. You are intoxicated by a volume of alcohol not comprehensible yet you are still coherent. That the world is now ascribed to other forces, the subconscious of the mind is the very element's fantasy, fascination – it is of course the laws of physical science are not; that you cannot leave this place by waking up because you are already awake brings horror with icy teeth.

The fourth circle

It is here in a small eddy of profusion that one finds the wild part of psychosis … the clitoris the same as the pineal. Its centre I suppose … the beast is not, at least not in the same way. As with human beings they are the most inaccessible places. It was the sum total of seventeen years of curiosity to come to this place and afterwards I found the need of the journey fully realized. This place harboured the power of the states, its pulse – I write as if I had gone along and in finding something picked it up. But this is not entirely true, rather it is my affection for the place. What was there was black and electrically storming and when I realized that none of the circuitry and context of mundane life would operate there yet the basis of being and individuality continued; I was fulfilled and delighted. This place bore wilful violence in such a resilient, resonant way that one was given the dark voices of dark things and without any meagre ration. It was as if violence and scenery were the same thing and the intensity of contact was one that took 40 lbs from my frame in a period of only some weeks and shot my metabolic rate through the roof.

I have discovered life, sentient life a black erupting storm in the shape of a volcano … walks by a silver-white ibis asleep on an equally enormous mountain of clear ice – this seems in storm too, electrically so and the more the storm the more the ice propagates, like a gigantic gem. Above the volcano held there by the ferocity of the walking story is a cube of black steel of enormous proportions. Submerged in this is a myriad of faces which appear and submerge, appear and submerge and make the metal molten. It is some element in the air which is continuous about this cube and I can not splash down about the volcano but its resistance produces a humming in the form of a voice which is giving slow simple directions in a monotone on how to vacate your body for parts unknown.

It is surely I, but what of that? I know nothing of that yet. All I know is that I am a being awoken, yet I have not thought … thoughts are not for me yet and even the thought of thought.

The third circle

Here is the contradiction. A vision appears. It is of a woman, her tits are like banners, she is dressed in hardly any blazing red silk. She has a leather whip and flogs a man on the back. He can emit no cry or sound, but in the sound of the whip striking is the evoking of an era of peace, passion, fertility and normality. The vision changes to another. You watch as you in a future incarnation as the opposite sex are stripped and made love to on a beach. You become wildly aroused by yourself and fall in love.

This place is a machine which begets other machines. They attack you with what they are, with themselves, with their substance. It is that their device is infinite. How can one outthink a plethora of intricate devices which bear no definition and are indeed the landscape where you exist? It is that your mind will take a tiny thread like fibrous pus and proceed to withdraw it from the abscess. Still longer, still larger, the pus and fibre come from the leg; amid a torrent of passionless, pure physical relief arises a panic and terror. The voluminousness seems to suggest the flesh and viscera of the leg has been totally consumed leaving only a shell which will collapse. On the other hand this is a place, as any place is a place, with inhabitants whose intricacies if not accessible on a logical level, are accessible on an irrational one.

There is a great mastery of life available from the irrational. Its language is somewhat difficult but it is often the revelation and the delight that one is given as the seemly insoluble unfolds or presents its end equation in poetry on first enquiry. It is only the system of Western culture we live in that finds this language 'nonsense', and then again the very roots of this culture are of beauty of the irrational. I think of the bison and other works painted in caves in places such as Lascaux; of how they show that every relation and interrelation is not based on how life is seen to be or wished to seem to be, but truly what is. When one looks at this art one is given an absolute reality in a language that is always just outside the field of vision that dwells where the illumination from the light of the fire does not penetrate. It is this place that is still making our decisions for we have valued it so much as to not let it go.

The second circle

This circle is an intelligence that is incongruous. It is that to be here; one does not make that decision oneself but requires a like-mindedness. It is that the intelligence is so powerful and so undefinable that your own intelligence becomes riddled with cracks and fissures and places where the common does not meet the common.

It is here that you alter your mind in a way that is otherwise not available elsewhere. It is somewhat like having a never-ending conversation with the Selenite, that master intelligence of the moon with a never-ending pot of black, sweet coffee. The very beginnings of this discourse have long fallen away, dead ashes in a dead fire and no termination can not only not be calculated, it can in no way even be envisaged. All the while the electro-synapses are firing more and more. It is that you drain out the quantity that is reason from your brain and in its place is put the kaleidoscope which is accessible to thought and associated narrative.

The first circle

This place is not what you would expect, in a real sense. It can never be. While one finds what is here fraught with denizens of all kinds, so much so that one could spend lifetimes encountering them, they are never definable, immune to classification they totally destroy order. Also there is not a specific dimension on which they operate, a corner of wall or a piece of builder's scaffold, a piece of tyre, a faint but definite illusion in a darkened sky, casual visitors one can see through, solid figment, the unexplained restructuring of things, and so on … yet all share animation and perhaps hazard. Yet there is something else amid this, a rapport with angels. The intent to distil one from another meets with a vast crevasse. The angelic that is so possessing that one will gladly live with the other things that possess this place regardless of the aura of hazard and danger that becomes constant.

Things come and go, appearances become strobe-lighted commonplace and an orchestra of angels play bizarre brass instruments the gusts of air from such showing off their fine flaxen pussies as it seduces, their cloth finery above their waists, all whilst floating in a sea of adrenalin.

There is a seduction to this place, a razor-edged mania with a mouth that has never not had lipstick on and is vent to only one purpose, that the place can be put to order and thence a constructivist's pleasure can be derived. It cannot be done, that is how this place is bitter. On the other hand allegiances and hostilities change and so do the tolerances of human beings. One can find this place quite habitable and the angels angelic but it will always be that that fine channel in the psychic will be out of equilibrium and in some state of shock like one's balance when one has something wrong with the canals of the inner ear.

What we have here is perhaps the basement of this incalculable edifice, psychosis. I have seen intelligent and sensitive men and women fall asunder reaching for stars and angels in skies that do not exist. Rather one must dig through the floorboards and at the most alacrious pace possible, for then the hazards are less that one will be eaten by some creature of trauma.

It is in the basement that the party is, and it is in full full-frontal swing … in the corner under an ultra-violet light is an angel bare except for very sheer tight coffee-mist stockings held up by a miniscule lace garter belt … she is more bone than she could possibly be just nude, unclad, moist, open, odorous of a score of smells, sweaty, a tart, a whore, a trollop and a harlot all rolled up into one, she is without eyes, only dark ponds of shadows where you can see the reflections of the forest and fire, when you see the wet, pure vermillion mouth you are transfixed, intoxicated and addicted, and the serotonin and dopamine surge and flow erratically – this is where you get your first blow job. It is the admission to madness, meanwhile the party is in full swing. Beside her is a Rakshasa with lizard-green skin and eight breasts like a sow.

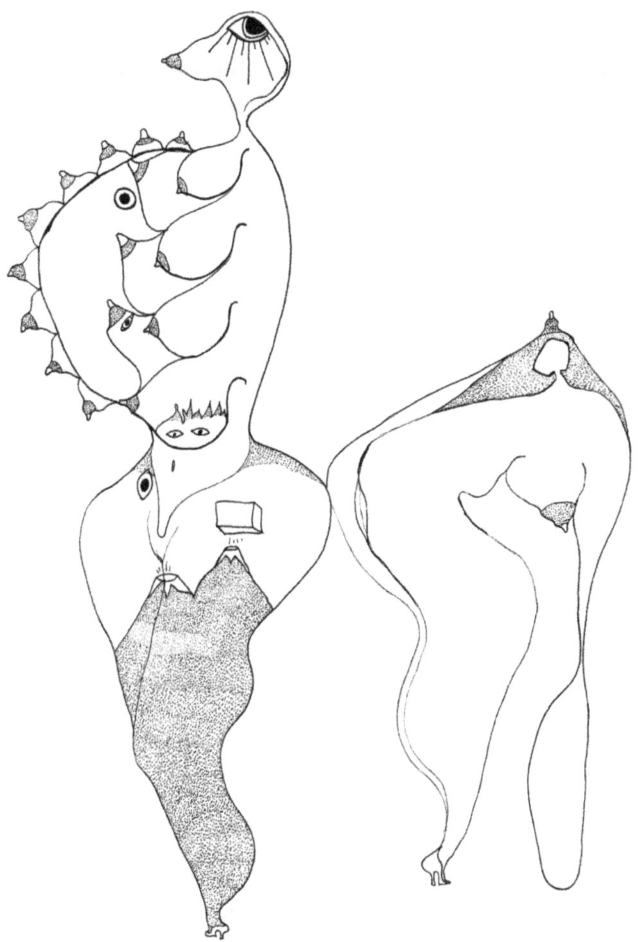

This started off as an inoffensive bank teller and it was the obsessive urge to possess more and more that made it this way and now it is on one hundred and nineteen different kinds of hormones, at least that is the story it would wish you to believe. In reality it was created that way and is one of the deadliest of all creatures, watch out!

In the adjacent corner are visionary 'things', I can't quite make out what they are, it would need a thorough examination, sort of translucent things made from colours that are a failure of an artist palette, imbued with some kind of mechanistic occult force, they are mugging an angel for what seems no reason whatsoever … one of her cute red high heels has spun across the room.

The room chatters and dances as things both become more disparate and merge so thoroughly that there is absolutely nothing remaining. A sort of feeling best described as disbelief comes upon one when one tries to find one's way out to go home – the party just gets bigger and everything expands in order to let it be, and there is no exit.

It is an interesting structure this seven circles with the beast huffing and puffing in the centre but no truer than anything else, but then again no falser. But before you feel that I have taken you for a ride I will have to again say that there is no structure or definition with this place I am writing about, only experience and therefore the truth of it is not muddled or obscured by games about how many doors it has or whether the windows are clean or not.

Mad women are unusual in bed. Never a passive moment and the oscillation is head-splittingly rapid. At one pole she is so enamoured that her vital signs indicate her life support is on the brink of possible permanent collapse and at the other that she is the unwilling victim of a homicidal attack. There may be some sort of domestic reflection to be sought here but in this case oscillation from pole to pole is continuous and within the span of seconds. It definitely gives the European allusion to 'spice' in a coupling substance. It's as if the madness isn't just confined to a part of the cranium but becomes so liberal (you are mad also, of course) that you transfer worlds between each other and propagate them as you exchange body fluids and the elixir of life.

I left her on the bed and went to smoke a cigarette on the sofa. As the cigarette haze began to permeate the room I could detect a slight difference occurring to her, rapid but almost imperceptible changes. She was lying naked and on her back with her legs open with a twist of cotton sheet across her stomach, she looked like she was giving birth. Slowly arising from her vagina came a luminous haze which developed into a contorted ectoplasm that began to give forth garbled sounds.

As I watched fascinated and the cigarette burnt to the end unattended it conquered vowels, monosyllables, words, finally speech:

“What am I doing here,” it said.
“Don’t ask me, I’m just looking.”
“Something isn’t right, I can’t get free.”
“Perhaps you’re not meant to. After all you’re her madness.”
“It would be nice to be independent.”
“She won’t let you go, she loves you, besides it isn’t worth it, you’ve got the best of all possible hosts, she lets you do whatever you wish, I know, and quite possibly if you did try to make it on your own you’d be terminated on some nondescript therapist’s couch …”

With the conversation finished I helped myself to another cigarette, then caught the ectoplasm’s attention and asked a few meaty questions of my own about its host’s turn-on buttons and other useful information. She was never the wiser and cursed me in the morning before setting about her way as usual.

It so readily comes about that there is a cross-over in language and terms between the myriad of landscapes. A visionary grasp that comes from chaos might well be almost completely represented by the oil painting on the wall in the bare wooden Kafkaesque room that you might find yourself within while partaking some psychotic experience. It’s all very well to subdivide and demarcate experience, to list things, confusion, disorientation, disorder, chaos, but these differentiations are intellectual and only carry a certain limited amount of power and utility. In the end one is reduced but not in an erroneous way to very rudimentary basics for survival. Awareness of a scope that is integral with the vision, intuition, and the capability to reconstruct the parts of yourself asundered in the contest in a more flexible way.

The moon in chaos, the sun in fragments, Jupiter vanished as if abducted, Neptune in never-ending deluge, the moons of the solar system turning frantically on their own axis, the rings of Saturn transfixed by Pluto, Uranus an ice-cube that has dropped out of the heavens and shattered somewhere below, the Earth and Venus in incest, the endless burning passion erasing all time, Mercury that has split. We are dealing with the enormities of personal cosmology and truth in these places, where they are not invention as it's used in the vernacular for that is reduced to rubble in the first cataclysm, and there are many, they happen constantly, but invention with its essence and sheer power, and mystery that will take of the other worlds, the netherworlds, the underworld and make anything it likes. Indeed, the holocaust the demented possess is their mental workshop.

Society gives bad rendering to the lunatic and maniacs that exist within its need for realism. The visionary buys you nothing unless you market it through society's infrastructure as say, Colin Wilson did, or unless there is a fine mystique which is romance in another form, such as with Carlos Castaneda and his books. As for the unconscious it is best left in book form on some psychologist's shelves for it is far too awesome and deadly to even open, much less touch, no better still, let's forget all about it.

Phillip Heckenberg is one of the fine people making art brut in Australia. It seems that he has spent the most part of the last two decades in the low security prison that is the mental hospital. He makes good art, mostly line drawings that inevitably involve the erotic, god and the nude. All three seem quite happy together, albeit the transcendental motive is a black anguish, that would do justice to a Coptic priest of last millennia. Amid the shuffle of priestly robes though is something else again, it is an immense and all-pervading beast that is always in the same room as him, tapping his shoulder here, tapping his shoulder there, bringing his attention to this, bringing his attention to that. The beast is called 'Voyeur' and is possibly the spirit of one of the great pornographers and it reveals every abomination and subtle nuance while Phil sits on his throne and casually adjusts his robes.

Anthony Hopkins is a different kettle of fish, or rather, bowl of light. Discontent to settle for seeing the mundane as reality, he decided at some stage to see the souls of things. It's what verses all his works. Space orbs, wizard lights, psychic lights, the souls of stars, all receive documentation with the coloured pencil, and most importantly, affection. It is that along with the classification and render goes a warm handshake for being so patient. Others don't see these things in life, or if they have access speak about them speculatively and unsurely. Those things which are close afoot are the para-psychological studies involving Kirlian photography and the psychic's contemplation of the aura.

These are luminous people who have built true cosmologies for themselves independently of society's wishes that it only be accepted as source. Those that can bring into being the most powerful and subtly precise cosmologies knowing invariably that there is another gravity are the true exponents of invention.

I had great aspirations for this place chaos and was in no way disappointed – I found more than was possible to retrieve and I am a master of this, but what impact? I have hazy recollections of people photocopying fractal dot patterns endlessly and speaking excitedly about concepts and theory – it was like having someone wanting to discuss the varying incidentals of your army's weaponry while you are facing the might of another army and preparing a mounted offensive.

None of these philosophers cared to come near its precipice, its denuding, quickening chaos and if they had it would have blown their papers to smithereens. My lost, however, was to enjoin others who had had the journey to this place and it remained a loss. It gradually became evident what I already knew, that I had gone to these places full of ferocity and brought back something of it with me. Undoubted there are those living in cheap back flats and flop-houses, émigrés to the country and those that have just 'gone away' who have been to and from chaos and have a knowledge common with mine about its landscape.

… I seem to be in a place … that is better than yesterday … there was no place yesterday only violence in motion, as if it was a living, breathing inhabitant of this place I was encountering … it led me down into some sort of chasm this morning … this place is beyond one's wildest dreams … I could describe it in minute detail just from the experience in my body. I have been awake since the day before yesterday and I haven't moved because of an extreme fever for ten days now, except for the bathroom of course. I can still manage that … haven't eaten in two weeks, must be greatly dehydrated.

I have been trying to name this chasm … it doesn't need a name though. I know it's called the chasm of doors … all ceased when I entered it … I have been going deeper and deeper into it … I do not want to stop and look, it will waste time and I want to see what is at the bottom … I have only so much time here … travelling is very hard, this place seems to be charging me my soul … early morning broke on this place today, I saw it as a vast vagina of violent volcanic ashes, infinitely dangerous but if travelled correctly, one of the moons of the esoteric cosmos … this morning I ate a little vegetable but brought it up … the fever is at its height and I cannot walk.

… I had a very clear vision of the moon tonight which is unusual for I could not possibly see it from where I am lying on the floor. It was before my eyes and seemed to be composed of sections of dried cuttlefish skeleton which gave it an unknown fragility. It was untouchable if it was to stay intact. It came closer and closer and regenerated into the pale cuttlefish, luminous with life … I did not know that I wanted such a thing with its confusion of tentacles so close to me.

… I took this waterous vision of the moon to be the harbinger of the death-knell of the spirit of my being … I will have to hurry into the chasm at a great speed now … I can no longer find adjectives, the place is beyond it. I am accepted by it also in an absolutely impersonal way … but I will have to hurry, my body will give me only a certain amount more of time … already I am continuously six months on this journey, and ferociously … I am at the lowest point of this place … there is a making of sound about me I cannot describe … I am lying on the heart of this place and in every way dimension is defied.

There was a major eclipse of the moon last night although it was kept a hidden thing, obscured by heavy rains and the watery-coloured glares of the city into the cloud. So much more for the good then if the arcane is about his full eclipse. You feel more in the dark, darkness precludes the logical rationalization the modern human regards as all for the passage through life and allows that more ancient sensory empathy to occur. If it had been a starry night this incongruity would have been a picturesque happening available to picture-postcards and the like. As it was, it was wiser affecting a great many things about human beings obscurely with the silence of a portentous thing, like a sculptor who with great concentration removes the last piece of stone from a work although indeed, he is told by others, the piece is already complete and he does this in a silent catacomb. Picking up the piece of fallen redundant stone he finds it a piece of honey-combed moon.

It is this 'modern mind' which is an injurious thing. It feels it should answer all the questions itself and then to the point that they can be neatly filed away labelled 'actioned'. What is more it demands substance, logical substance, and verification, logical verification. Even if dealing with intuition and awareness, it is felt not quite right unless there is an accompanying sheet of data or a sign in the sky. That mind is injurious because it is deft, it has learned how to put the round peg in square hole.

Also last night I attended a benefit film night for U.F.O. abductees. The first thing I liked was the appearance of a Mr Peter Khoury who named himself as one who had been abducted by extraterrestrials. I liked his speaking. It was obvious that his mind had made great leaps since his experience and not because of some extraterrestrial implant or technology but because his consciousness and unconsciousness wish to gain the stature to be mobile with an experience that he said had no 'rationale'. Finding absolutely nothing 'factual' to feed the modern mind he grasped another reality of awareness as well.

Everything seems to have lost its definition, it's night but it doesn't feel like night. It doesn't feel like day either, it doesn't feel like in-between, it just feels different. This is beyond my relative experience of time and place. There is a tremendous noise – din, cacophony, confusion, commotion – it is like my life is blowing away – there are the sounds of steel girders being torn loose, of the clatter of things not properly secured, or needless being blown in front of a wind that is ferocious and relentless and the sound of the Akashic record in my ears like the scream of a creature that can't be contemplated.

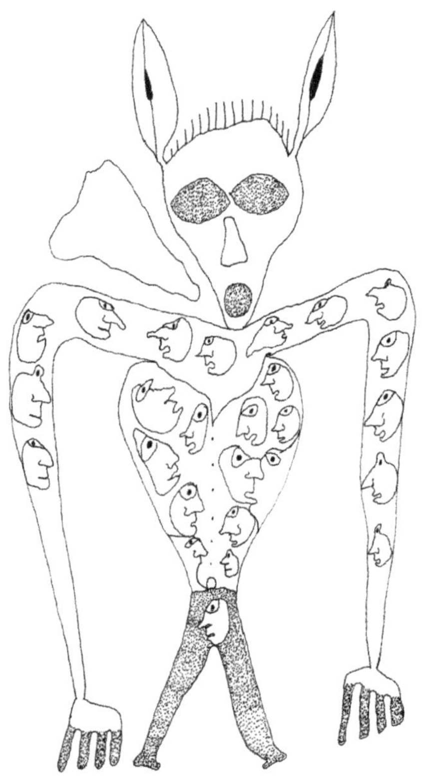

There is a light it defies every description, more so it defies every feeling of the way I know reality, and yet this is reality – it has been months now since I talked to anybody, just a chance meeting with a friend, months since I slept in a bed, but I don't think of these things – I am too intent on my destination, that is the only way that I will eventually be there. It is like a journey through a great alien body.

Tony,

Upon reflection:

Your description of the 'core' as an all-pervading 24 hour-a-day, non-stop lightning storm of pure white pulsating energy that at the same time is beyond all description that at the same time is 6-sided & can be manipulated corresponds, or seems to, exactly with the all-pervading white light energy that the Tibetans call Void or Mind – only which from time to time, for a few brief moments, I have also experienced. Hope you don't find the above 'wording of it' presumptuous. It's a note to thank you for a very exciting evening & for your excellent feed-back on my own 'poetic' explorations.

See you soon, Phil

There is a certain 'ethic' in the schizophrenic trek. It's that one gets to one's destination if one doesn't bemoan the altered consciousness and non-rationale of the journey.

The two 'destination' and 'non-rationale' seem to sit a little sorely with each other but it is an expansion we are talking about, an enriching of the way everything is. Strangely, there are seemingly inconsolable parties, an absolute pointlessness which the Europeans call 'pointenlose Konsequenz'[46] married with an unyielding drive; an absolute fixed point that everything else will be sacrificed for.

It is that with psychosis there is a disco-ordinate expansion of reality making readily possible the working, and competently so, of direct oppositions. In terms of our desire for imbued human dynamics we should be enjoining not curing.

The ethic I speak of is the same regard one gives a well-worn and trusty old car that with affectionate handling will make the trip and after all, at some stage and some place, some time, there was at least feeling for a trip, and in this car room, to passage various important items, friends, companionable creatures and the odd alien or two. Start kicking the car and it will turn on you like a pack of ravenous timber wolves.

In one way being in the car driving along through strange territory mapping and exploring and coming into contact with both the strangely and humorously bizarre (also the beautifully bizarre) with every passenger seat filled with an 'imaginary' comrade that long ago has become far in excess of real is all that is wanted but the resistance for this by logic and its purveyors and policemen is always of magnitude.

7.6.93
Sydney

I have been thinking a few things about Davey Brown lately. David disappeared from public view about 1988. Possibly he returned to England – he was originally from Liverpool. Phillip Hammial and myself came upon Davy at Rozelle Hospital, a psychiatric hospital in Sydney, during 1985. He seemed to be an unloved character by the hospital. He purported to know everything about words and this was regarded as some sort of extreme arrogance by the hospital staff – he didn't even wear a suit and tie.

What he did possess was an inescapable mania of the mysticism and associative symbolism of words and their components, so much so that they would talk to him. With this went forty-five complex and large graph sheets with words interwoven and broken down to different coloured letters. With this also went an erotic and astounding knowledge of a kind of semiotics of the irrational that obviously could come only from a very intense vision.

When one spoke to him at length he would let you in on the secret and that was all it took and you would be entranced into his cosmology where words did what they were supposed to but had a secret function as well, and a personality, and an identity.

Davey's 'sheets' were exhibited by the Australian Collection of Outsider Art in 1987, and I remember a man in a short-sleeved suit with a tie and shaven head that had just been polished, animated beyond content and flinging his arms about and saying repeatedly, 'don't you see, don't you see'. Or the other end of this discourse was a professor of semiotics from one of the universities who was in a fervour of excitement and who was on the precipice of his logical and historical knowledge about words looking into their irrational mysticism and beaming, but still holding onto his ground for dear life.

ROSEY SPITE

'Whether buying a shipment of the fine cigars she smoked in Havana and being personally hosted by Fidel or off on a secret journey to Seville, Spain with a confidential plan to uncover a lost case of Edward VII whisky and motoring the back road there in her 1929 jalopy, Rosey Spite is undoubtedly herself.'

I never met Rosey Spite, it was just that she was spontaneously there. I happened to be having a few drinks in a hotel in Glebe, Sydney. I was in the engine room again. All these nuts and bolts of grey dissonant karma I was sure that could be got at and quite possibly for profitable usage. To suggest this place, the jute box was rife with that atonal pop song and there were screams, yells, cheers, arguments and laughters. A suited gentleman made himself known and joined my table. He asked why I was in this hotel I told him it was to find some peace and quiet; he couldn't comprehend and 'baaa-ed' his way elsewhere. Meanwhile I went on dismantling engines, great big grey monstrosities that had been vibrating and jolting me down a subterranean passageway that was becoming smaller and tighter and no passageway at all in an effort to find the stop button. This particular voyage was already ten constant weeks in progress.

I paid for another beer and sat down. I looked out the window and there was myself walking down the street with Rosey Spite beside, we were discussing. At that time the scenery was of a 'fantastic' quality as of the architecture of Rudolf Steiner, little houses with demeanours that seemed to come from a German forest and a street that was obviously meant to be walked. Rosey wore a pin-stripped black suit with cravat with a diamond pin and black short hair slicked back and she had a prominent short bird's beak. I was in khaki knickerbockers with a red floral Hawaiian shirt and on my bare head a dozen tuffs of radiant ginger hair erupted. We went back to my place to discuss finding the central nervous system of the engine room. Rosey had great plans, she felt we should take over the whole ship and plunder it, that we would never have an opportunity like this again.

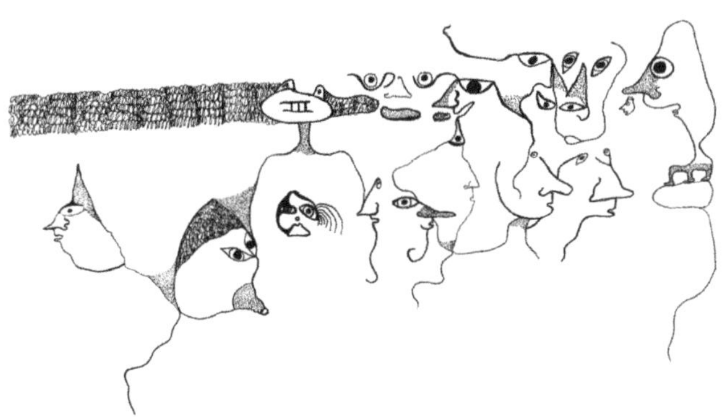

Rosey expressed a strong interest in the room full of heads that I kept. It was in this catacomb that I would often sit and as they screamed and ranted and raved and recanted their deeds of horror in horrific manner I would speculate on a greater self and a gentler world. The horror of this place mattered not to me, in fact I found it relaxing. I would often admit Rosey here and she would calmly and adroitly question them to see if perhaps it were possible for them to go elsewhere where they'd be happier.

The winds about me didn't so much abate with Rosey's coming as change their character. While remaining just so harsh the desolate, unliveable, the caustic gave way to the searing infectious desert wind that knew every vernacular and dialect and often after rain there would be a cornucopia of the most bewildering and absurd humour. In mood I was in constant oscillation between the darkest terror to the most sublime and distended humour from the things

I saw. But it was at this point that I did start to become a magician, and a black one at that. When I talk about black I mean the places I ventured not the nature of my heart. Besides Rosey would allow only a certain number of demons into the house and then no more. She never acquired my complacency in dealing with the profusions that used to arrive from the Underworld and many, many other places and used to retire to her quarters after giving them a cursory inspection. She was however invaluable with neighbours who at this time plagued me – 'You saw what? With how many arms?' No, probably only a figment.

I decided to practice magic upon the heads. It was that the mouths of these heads were never silent. I began to compose a music with them. It was that I could find in these symphonies, each head being an instrument, the great sagas, the great passions. I fell into them as a weighted body slips below the surface of an absolutely still and crystalline water. It was here in this cool place that I could hear everything that was about their voices and what they were saying. Combined in the expanse and throes of music they made one golden head with which I saw the ever-varied, the ever-repetitious and the ever constant. It was that I began to see pictures, that I travelled on a fine chariot to places and it was pulled by a great golden head. It gave forth music and arias and singing as we went from one place to another seeing the workings of the very illusion itself. It was that I would often encounter more heads in dimensions and realities that differed greatly between themselves and as with the bevy of heads I first came upon in the room, they all became part of the one thing and outlandish as this was it be a familiar and loved thing. I came upon a luminous being. He was no surprise to me, I often travelled with a small luminous being that was known as small T.V., however, also I was utterly surprised. He came from an unfathomable place, attracted by the music. This was a delight for to find him otherwise would have involved journey to a place where one cannot keep one's mind.

It has long been the associative narrative of psychotic thought that has interested me. When I came upon the philosophy of Heraclitus as reality of flux as all of the river and all at once I feel there is a knowing about this narrative which is outside of the bound of what one can understand if one gives discourse with it or involvement. There are so many places with this flux yet it's all the same water, so many acrobatic tricks, so many spontaneous possibilities that were not before, so easily are things, disconsolate things welded and how elusive this river's creatures that might evolve or devolve through myriad incarnations and orders of life until one has a monster of the far flung future to contend with or the infinitesimal speck that still has something of life in it that the monster has become.

So often the conversation becomes a sort of natural poetry – one of the visions to conceive is how in the intricacies of language one travels a vast structure of escalators making continuous connections and journeys and with an almost theatrical series of digress exit at precisely the same point to the precise footstep, of entry.

This is a mandala in the hands of a virtuoso who carries a briefcase loaded with dynamite who regards what he is doing as his normal daily affair. Encased with subtle coercions and brutal absence a lunatic within a maze, he will not gradually wander his way out to a host of applauding psychiatrists but will digest it like a madman and have a party belching, farting, sneezing and picking his nose. I spoke of Davey Brown and his 'sheets'. It seemed to me after I had gone to see him again and again that his creation – all the bones of the English language, bones that make a living luminous creature that one might have a discourse with must have come about from a knowing that is beyond knowledge albeit somewhat like an expectant father. Davey must have spent what seemed to him an endless time imbibing mania, coffee and cigarettes. When I think of him I see a black and white photograph, he is standing there the proud parent, beside him the unconscious and also his offspring, his cosmology of how the English language is, which can be discovered in no other way than he has done. It is playing marbles at his feet.

What seems at first to catch and then astound with the natural poets of madness is how paradox becomes a malleable thing, how even sometimes like a trained but wild circus animal it will perform effortless impossibilities. But there are those things of the wilds that hunt too, and that circus animal can take the head off his owner with one swipe, whoosh! Nevertheless, there are the singing canaries and the trained seal that can balance adverbs on its nose, the furry dog that will leap endlessly and tirelessly through the hoop and much more of everything. When expression fails with a circus like this on the road then we have a life or death situation. What point to having the apparatus to take anything apart or put anything together when there are no raw materials, no shipment of dissembled nuts and bolts to send off to China in trade for cases of joss sticks or no shipment of wiry new gadgets devoid of instructions to put together and parade down the street …

… Although one thing seems to accompany this circus and its retinue, the thing that makes the dematerialisations and rematerialisations possible through the maze of paradoxical indices and that is an inward brutality that sets the madman apart; without this quality the circus cannot be paid, without it it would run to wrack and ruin.

This brutality the madman uses first and foremost on himself, it is a way to see when all else fails – there's no knife like a sharp knife and applying it to oneself sweeps away every illusion, what remains is a ground you can stand upon. When used on others it is devastating, but it has no point in this manner.

It has a more 'seemly' application, at least by the conventions of society and a landscape – that is what it is, brutality, a place.

The art brut makers who ply their trade inexorably have a contact with the unconscious that is not widespread and one thinks should give vent to elitist and other concerns which would gradually impair their sight. But here the knife comes in. In a paring away of the redundant, of the social, of the emotionally unnecessary, one gets closer access to the beast and is freer with it, and the beast is rewarding.

This direct relationship with the unconscious is what fascinates, always has since I learned such a place existed and it was possible to exchange with it. When one looks to a lunatic one immediately comes into a plethora of another reality. By lunatic I mean it in its original meaning of lunacy, one that has fallen asleep in the light of the full moon, and all of it is within. There are many moons involved here, some as black as sin, others awesome in eruption, others diaphanous and enigmatic, yet others constantly in metamorphosis but the stamp of the unconscious is upon them, they are all the moons that revolve, orbit, pirouette, vaporise and emerge about this landscape that is the unconscious. When I see Anthony Hopkins' drawings of round balls of startling and friendly but somewhat addictive life I immediately see the moons that have been overhead in places I have travelled in the unconscious, places that bear no similarity with other places.

The relationship I have had with the place has always been one of escalating multiples, of multiplicities, intrigues and intricacies; disassociated from a view of the simple and sweet things of the place alone, instead of enmeshed, my desire has always been paramount and fanatical to reach the core of the unconscious via psychosis and chaos. In the paradox having gotten to the core of the irrational I doubt that it has one. Rather, the place therein is an entity within which there is landscape, colour, and yet other entities and natural forces that have intelligence … rather, it is a landscape peopled and there is absolutely no definition for this peopling … rather, it is a realm that entitles all and includes all when one is with it … rather still, it is a living beast that moves and changes constantly and you are within it … rather and also it is awareness, vision and material and they are ever-changing to make what they wish and these things are what compose you.

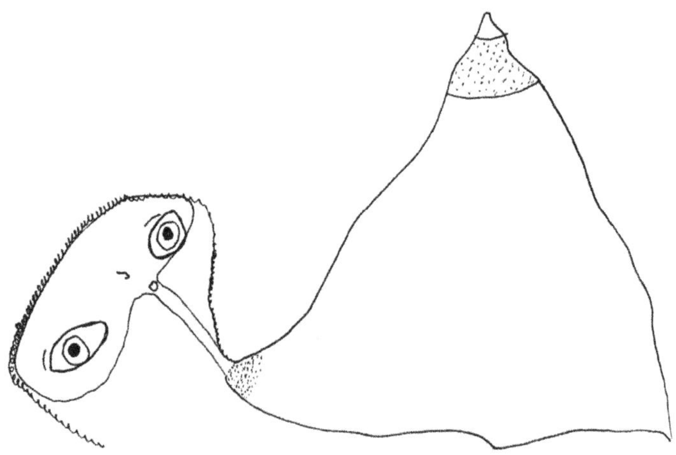

What is interesting about madness is the alien it makes one. Once separated from conventional reality one retains the act of separation whether one curses a 'sickness' or embraces with eyes open a very separate reality. It is that you have experienced a place the majority have not although they are aware that it is there, they have noticed its power also, and no amount of letter writing will suffice to communicate the feel of this place. There are other things in this being an alien also.

… he came through the door rather than into the room and more materializing than entering … there was a four-fingered hand growing out of his forehead, it had no thumb and was trying unsuccessfully to snap its fingers. I gathered from this appendage that firstly attention was required and secondly, that he was trying desperately to remember something important, perhaps the secret of life. He would recur and reappear often and always with an invincible entrance and always different, his bizarre physical manifestation changed as readily as the stock market.

I was always in great interest as to why I came about to journey in these extraordinary realms. For many years amid an overwhelming fanaticism to be there, what intuitively seemed absolutely true was that I was a modern-day Job in a bible of a very different sort.

I discovered an old photograph of myself at twelve years of age, dressed dapper and at a Catholic Holy communion.

I am in communication with this Christ beside me – we have made a pact to do and experience everything illicit that there is. Already my eyes have that absolute comprehension of sin and an incalculable knowingness, observers can see this precisely but they cannot penetrate behind the eyes no matter how hard they try.

Already I am seeing strange creatures

in strange places

and calculating

how to get there.

The Universe is something unerring; part of this, the planet, is unerring, we also, excepting when we go against our true nature but what is made by this antiphony feeds the chaos of the universe ... that which is central to its own being and we are given call to take from it and make it into our own way.

See me in the face, my body is buried. I am wanting and wanted. Are you he? He left taking his luggage and mine. I will not allow you to pair what is in my face … ever more intricate and ever more involving, beseeching, monopolising, whingeing – the debate with the rational mind becomes; it is like the analogy of finding lucidity in the many coloured lights of the streets, it is one thing I suppose.

"In places there is the most erudite blackness and screaming. Yet what people withdraw from in terror is both sensuous and erotic beyond limit. Mind you to indulge is to finish, at least temporarily, in a horror. Out of such a thing a certain will forms like an iron crystal that is so remarkable, it is a gem."

The conversation begins somewhere in a woman's twenties, the one above, how she was buried, its details, the possibility of excavation, are lost already and the rational will go on talking about the fact for the next sixty years. This great pointless literature of human beings is surely an indictment of where we have placed our reason, our cause, where it is buried, and an awesome revenge by an irrational that will never let itself be subjugated.

I am thinking of George Karnikowski. George gives credence to this world and I don't, it is the source of the 'lively debate' between us. Notwithstanding, there is another way he sees this absurdity of rational things and that is with his drawings. To go to his modest home and see his artworks laid out (he deals with visitors to his home any way but modestly – still as potential buyers in a marketplace where he has an art brut picture drawn in his mind) is like visiting the baubles of Cartier's. There before you are all the gems of rationality, they have been carefully plucked from the eyes of the demons that possess them. (Now, once possessed) and set in new opulent findings and mountings in a way that makes both the alien and unordinariness of the irrational beautiful. I think the beast is very pleased in him. So this rational-mindedness drives us crazy with its lack of consequence and heartlessness, that we know, but its real device is that it separates us from the core, it offers us fragments.

It is no enigma that many embrace a chaotic mind that comes from an impersonal pureness to remove a logic that has gone wrong and that they fall in love with it when they find it faithful and performing. To be involved in part with this chaos is to be involved with it all – it is a place that bears no divisions.

9.6.93
Sydney

When one is pursuing the conquests of landscapes of places you might term irrational, unreal or illogical one is not available for accountability, at least not in the social term we give it. In these journeys and spaces the action of responsibility is absolute, but it is to oneself. It is the nature of what is to be lost and what is to be gained that makes it so. It is no place for others to see some sort of reflection of themselves remonstrating their logic of emotional problems. Leave the lunatic alone, give him what he wishes and needs, an arena to be centurion, to be general, to be historian and poet, to be tactician … these incursions into the unconscious have their armies, have their cities that are fought for and against with every resource, the stakes are high, these are cities of the self, it is as likely to lose as to win and there is no such thing as conquest without hardship. The option of who and what of the self is to live and who and what is to die is a constant companion, each journey is particular and there are no maps to unexplored territory. In this, those that come with a self-righteousness based on their own perspectives to tell you that you are frightening them by not being like them, and that you are 'sick' and 'ill' are unwanted and very dangerous. The tactics of journey must be included to keep this wolf from the soul.

Beyond this, the specific and the emotional intermeshing comes the pure artistic word like an inestimable monument; what is is a sweeping concern that firstly levels all criticism that is before one, then levels all voice, including one's own. Chaos is not a force to be exploited, all concern for purpose is not only redundant, it is useless, futile. One's manner with it is always how to survive and next how to put the tools and implements to what it is about. That there is no objective in this is natural to it but not to you.

People are in error when they see madness as an affliction – it is great gifts at great prices. Even the act of attempting to comprehend the irrational, the unintelligible, for which there is no comprehension is an exercise in consciousness raising with a medium that is volatile and unlimited. It is the constant destruction that must compete with the incoming awakenings and acquisition of talents and not vice versa … but that destruction is awesome and unpredictable and can easily shake the core of those about one. Why go down into the pit? … and after that yet another and another. It is because one ends up owning them. They and their resources become part of the Realm one is establishing in the unconscious … Meanwhile, the centre of one's being falters between life and death.

I guess the thing that made me tackle the chasm was the fact that I had been a criminal in my early youth. I learned with this livelihood what it was like to be capable of anything. It was also when I developed a thirst for the word 'plunder'. I was recalcitrant and incorrigible. I made my entrances with more adeptness than a ferret and with more deviousness than an assassin. Always intrigue and the darker side of things were about these things. My favourite place of entry was a coffin factory, wherein inside I would recline inside a coffin and smoke a cigarette and while the adrenaline of illicit dealings was pumping within me, dream of Transylvania and the spirits of the dead. The chasm seemed like an easy mark. I didn't know what was inside but it was easy to get into and that is ninety percent of the problem solved.

I was careful who I selected to go in with me – I chose Rosey Spite, and Tiberia, the little voice that rode, Untuck, one of the minor spirits of the death.

Now I picture the place as the female sex organ – it had that wildness about it, it was impossible to estimate, for great periods of time as one experiences it there was nothing except the obsessive compulsion to go deeper, ever deeper. Rations were short, the place was never-ending, smouldering chunks of basalt loosen under Untuck's hooves and fell to a depth I could not comprehend much less fathom, I began to call the place the Chasm of Doom.

It was an arduous journey that broke some things and not others. Untuck, though small was relentless and he carried the sound of what we were about. It was the unceasing din at its bottom when we finally reached it that seemed most … important. Each heard what they wished, it was never-ending, it was blinding, expanse, incapable of being divided, broken down, vivisected, it was a whole, of which there are few …

I remember a great wind. I was saying goodbye to Samantha and it was right, that elegant balminess of late summer seemed cinemimatic, of an excluded dimension, appearing at no more than the cracks of this wind, this black wind blowing everything in my life away was murder itself. I was going to kill something, to execute something, killing things always made me insane, the act makes immeasurable sense but none at all, the last thing I saw was Sam's blond face like a lantern and then I was filled with murder.

SPIRITS

It seems that after seeing a great many of them it becomes obvious that no order or classification exists – there are no categories in which to place them all and therefore any attempt to make a structure with them will make nonsense within you … putting them in miscellaneous is dangerous, they are not meant for that, and so one regards them individually for what they bring into one's life, the intolerable, insanity, despair, illumination, power.

It of course was a spirit I was out to murder, everything else you can distract yourself from. How such a thing is done bears no cohesion, it's not of reality, it requires the investiture of the act, the will to do so, an absolute lack of compassion or patience and the power of insanity. I do not mean the floral state of madness, I mean the absolute barrenness of insanity – the instruments that scream in this place are not worth knowing.

… I butchered the body in the early morning sunlight, it was that sharp light that always reminds me of knives, there was not much of use … hard to say what afflictions this thing, it was only a thing now, had brought into my life, many I suppose, that was over, at least from this, wherever or whoever it had come from, I knew all of this before, but not now … I could feel the screaming in my head, and the morning looked like a wall of luminous paint in the dark.

It doesn't seem inconsistent to me that I should experience days of an overwhelming lucidity in the grounds of a mental hospital, if all the vestiges of the futile should develop laryngitis then this seems the place for it. It just shows you how wide sweeping and unlimited such a thing is when it can cart away the clozapine the doctors are giving you as well. However elusive I found this state, a heroic thing without need of weapons, the opposition to the feeling of life it brushed aside became obvious when before it was like a white man in white clothes against a white wall.

For a while I became acutely mediumistic, so much so that it was pathogenic. This separation from things had to be felt to be known and then something could be done. I was beset by the angst and irrationality mixed together of every casual passerby. What was more plaintive was that I could see the horrible places they were in and how unsubstantiated and imagined they were. It seems our prime occupation is building hells and our biggest gripe that no-one will share them with us.

Every morning I would clean up the myriad dirty footprints inside of myself and prepare for the next inundation. It was the feral irrational, that irrational that has no place to go that was the difficulty, everyone wanted to share it, exchange it: use it for currency. It came in faster than I could shovel it out, up the walls it went and up to the rafters, through the ceiling, I had absolutely nowhere to hang anything of my own. I became mad in a different way, I was seething on a dust of pure refuse. It was the useless mirror which showed nothing, this mirror of nonsense that was the impediment to the lucid sharp things I discovered – so when the weight of it broke something within me I put it out for the garbage man.

It is a lot easier to feel and know the things of life when you are a madman. It is the fact that life is not metered in mundane steps that are at artificial instance … moments are caught and become pliable for one.

Bob Dylan suggested something which points to this when he said one uses ideas as one's map. It is close; it is more that one uses, or chooses not to use landmarks, birthmarks, tender bruises, seeping wounds, all landscapes as they come into one's life and they have infallible entry.

We are composed of these things, a madman is a convulsion of them, it is his raison d'etre to be witness and lover to them … the rest of life pales in content compared to this … the static, the lies, the things that can grow nowhere because they don't exist.

It is society's misconception that lunatics are unprivileged people, that they are somehow handicapped with an incomprehensible negative …

… it is not so, in reality they are handicapped with an incomprehensible positive …

… almost as if they are an
evolutionary experiment for the future.

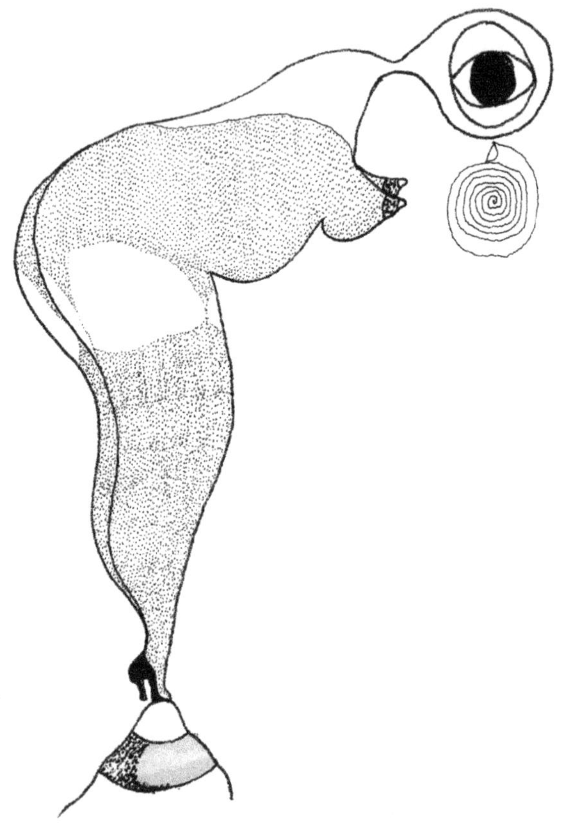

The Anima

the Persona

muse
the gap with the moon in its teeth.

In this place
which is one will find the presence of things
always indeterminate and
yet what is occurring is
equilibrium.

So much is happening and at such an accelerated pace that it seems everything is standing still.

What is constant is the FREEZING cold.

There is the obstacle with all his malice.

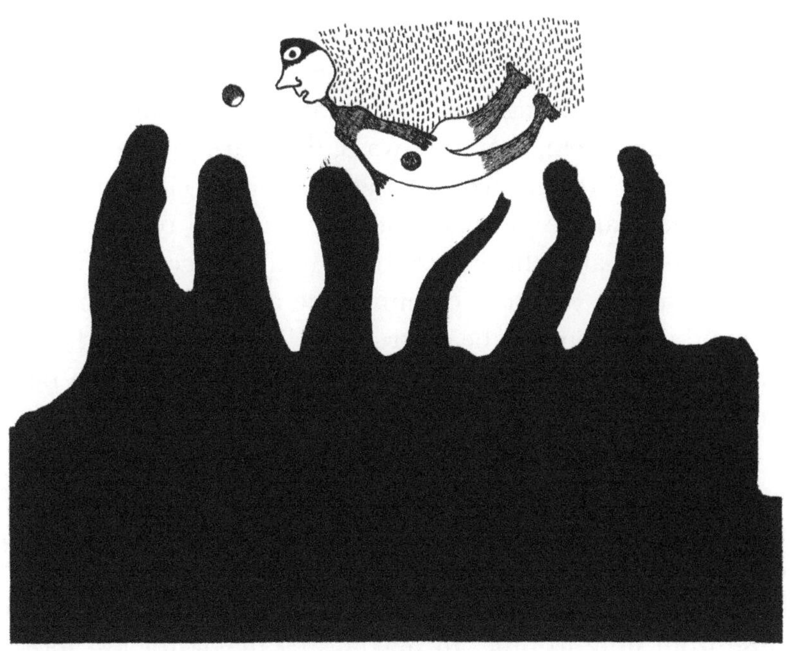

A host, of golden daffodils …
Wordsworth

This landscape of the Unconscious I have spoken of is my reason for being mad.

It's not available via any other experience. At best an extraordinary experience will put you in touch with it. It will show you it and that indeed is a very powerful thing but no other medium except madness will let you travel it, and then it must be an adept madness where one has access to the occultic, the psychic, the metaphor, prose-poetry, in order to survive it. One starts to gain dominion over this landscape when one starts to build with its resources instead of expiring upon its slopes.

THE OBSTACLE

… It is so often that things will occur that are irreversible. But that is only how they seem, there are ways, there are means. It is simple: if the things created that are precious come to ill and are broken, then they can be put back into the fires and recreated. The only thing that makes this impossible is indifference. It is first that you take away the obstacle, eliminate the assassin or their power (the same thing). Remove the obstruction. Then one should invoke magic. Magic finds its outcome more easily when there is a belief in what is to be than when there is not.

It has been a somewhat unusual day even though I slept the greater part of it. It is that I have had the pieces to build the piano for some time now and the music began today … the soft blacks, the sadness and sorrow, and melancholy. It is an affair of magic these boxes I realise from time to time. In making the magic for lost love or things irretrievably gone one must pay the price. I must commune with a piano with a siren's head for only she can give me what I want; meanwhile her music turns my heart black and threatens to sink it in a black sea.

I feel the box's music most from my feet. It sends every refuse that disheartens into my body. At times there are Chopin-like notes, perhaps Rosey has found a way to tap the line; at times I am nothing but erotic … Tiyana's psychic colleague says it was a great black insect from The Crevice and is the guardian of the Netherworld: Simon says I have formed a bond with a Rakchasa. I looked at my calendar for this year and find I am due to have a meeting with the beast of psychosis: is it possible I will at last get from it what I want?

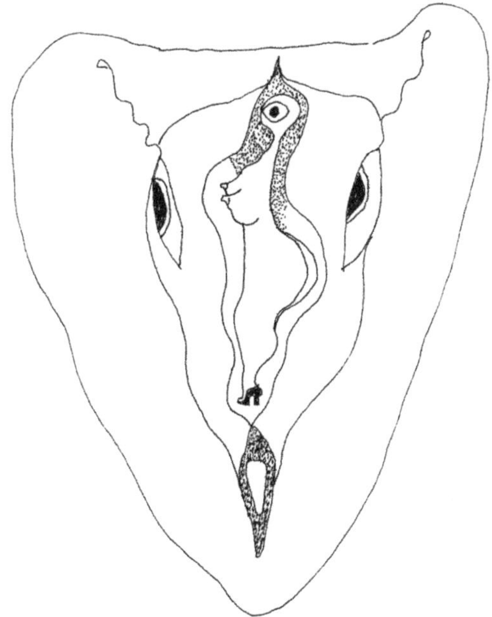

This place, THE OBSTACLE has been grinding its strength upon mine for months … I can think of nothing more than a countless barrage … the cold of an ice that should not exist and endless tearing by endless teeth, if my endurance was not paramount it would have ripped open a crevasse in my brain, that is where all its impact is felt. It is that I am traversing a place of inanimate, impersonal pain of extraordinary dimensions … still further in a recess within it is an intelligence which is opposed to mine, and it is this contest which is the core of things. I cannot but help thinking about Aleister Crowley and his writing about elementals whilst dealing with this thing … this ice bites like teeth that have made an impersonal study of hatred. It is something I do not have to defeat, it is wearing itself away on my patience and endurance as I cross it … at a given point in time it will be no more, simply something inside of me, something which I have devoured. Nevertheless for all of this I am in a pain, a purely physical pain and devastation that is extreme … in the morning I have my shower and if I close my eyes I can easily see that I am being flogged down the back and body by rapacious whips.

But then it is not all hard going this game of unconscious landscapes and madness; a lot of it is like groceries over the counter that the shop assistant forgets to charge you for … there are the endless avenues of thought that are so easy to travel and a guaranteed treasure down each one and nothing like a dozen or two of convivial hallucinations, entities, personas, creatures, shades, spirits and the odd ghost thrown in for good measure, such things when compounded make a visionary that is almost trite, yet that has an awesomeness on which you could break the spine of any fallacy and yet it is composed in a way that is almost ludicrous. It is another part of the landscape. It is its reverie, its d'oubli, where the forgetfulness of self and others is not irresponsible but a response to the intoxicating and drugged airs where one is … nothing more to do than sit there and imbibe the sensation of inspecting each grain of the schizophrenic trek knowing full well that they are mountains as well.

Perhaps the most splendid power one develops and one of the most powerful when one becomes a mad person is some constant discourse with the illogical, it becomes something that hands you revelations, constantly and integral with a situation rather than something that must somehow be decoded into the rational. It is a very powerful business being able to put together things which have no reason or equation. It takes the hand of a talented and practised artisan to do so. It offers now no description and that is how the artisan can say indisputably that they are an individual.

I am in a place, it seems there is nothing living here, no way leads from this place, there is great embargo. Utter hopelessness, yet my imprisonment in this place is only illusionary for what is keeping me here is my desire to know this place as one understands a lack, then it will be on my side, then it will be well. Me, I just have to find the right places to place my fingers and the right place into which to place my tongue. What does come to me day and night is the feeling that this place has never known walls or a pairing of any kind and the virginity makes up for its seeming desolation. Also I know that there is something with it, I am that practised at knowing where I am, I can feel it, hidden, a small luminous entity whom I call Small Radio, it is as if my body feels intimately the transmissions that he makes and is relentlessly hunting him, and he feels my coming with both timidity and the key to freedom, it makes the bareness illusionary.

I am in a place where there seems to be no light, this I find unusual, it is that I am well used to places of erudite blackness and yet if one is about these places it is that their blackness at least suggests the idea of light, here it is not so, even the very thought of light is unknown. The light that is myself is here somewhere, it makes no difference what vacuum of dimension puzzles me, I am too fervent about it to see the overwhelming intrigue such a place will place upon one.

It has always appealed to me that lunatics are people with special powers. It is over a decade since I made the acquaintance of Bob Pain in Ward 25 at Rozelle Psychiatric Hospital. The man was inescapable as a natural poet. The great histories and great books were plastic in his hands. He could construct a mysticism and epic of power out of the bible that couldn't be surmounted. When I heard him I believed in words again. He was the same age as me.

It's night. A full moon seems to make a contusion in a night sky wearing a lingerie of mist, there's a smoke from somewhere, at the cornice of my mind I feel an urgency about its fire, earlier I make a mistake thinking a projected spotlight on the cloud was the moon, it seemed like the clipped pelt that covers a woman's pubic mound, hardly noticeable but also blinding. The psychiatrists have it that more people go mad at the time of the full moon than any other: but their formulae are incessant ... more people go mad at the beginning of spring, presumably from the new year's pollen, more people go mad who show tendency to nervous behaviour ... with what we are presented in a lifetime how is it possible not to be nervous? As for me, I'll have my moon as the delightfully recurrent erotic filament it is, nobody is going to hang any saturnine foreboding on it for me, these quacks will just have to peddle their statistics down the road, preferably to the old woman at the end of the street who believes nothing and buys nothing. I am sure after our psychiatrists have dissolved we will still have our moon.

7.7.93
Sydney

I am in a place having a dialogue with a beast. In one of those momentary things the order of reality ... 'altered'. All processes took part, bending, compressing, vaporisation, evaporation, transpiration, violent cataclysm. I don't recognise the place but I do the beast, he is my old nemesis. It is years since I ceased to be his victim, now there is more joke than threat. It is strange being in such intimate relationship with one's torturer, but it has always been that way, it is as difficult for it being the torturer as me the tortured. At last he has run out of ploys, at last I am as wiry and as wry as he is. He is sitting still while I draw a picture of he, still talking and becoming greatly amused, for some reason he appears to disbelieve that I can capture his image, I, on the other hand, am absolutely certain of what I am doing, it is that from his inflections I know him better than any lover.

I am in a place, I should have known the beast better, because it is tortuous yet it is clean, like the combustion of coal. There is an honesty to the piercing of this place, it is that everything is intermingled with everything else and yet there is no confusion. It is in some way a relief that there is nothing living here, I knew that immediately, no fragile thing to care for and find, no horror to eliminate, what is here I can plunder ruthlessly without some trapping of a conscience, in that way it is honest, in that way it is clean. About me is a compacted mass, everywhere it is the same, this density, the place's own natural element is its weapon, the spirit in one is crushed out finally and devoured. Yet that tells me this place, it is nothing more than compacted energy, like coal, regardless of what cave-in or what rock-fall. There is a howling here as things compressed tighter and tighter and yet a silence for this place has no mouth. I feel I am embedded in some great sexual organ that needs a spark to ignite it.

I am in a place that seems a woman, such is the excitement. It is outlandish, everything grows here, everything is narcotic, psychotropic, carnivorous, open, moist, subservient, odorous, pulsing, swelling, every tree looks like a woman's sheer black stockinged legs, the place is growing by the minute, by the second, it is all mouth from some lost period in the cretaceous era and it is wrapped about me and yet this place is one of the most dire for it knows the tortures of a woman and yet is most impregnable for its life is the pleasure of a woman. Here the plunder will have to be subtler.

It is this idea of places that is superb. It is what the realists do not see, as if they are colour blind, talking to one about the realities of landscape one has known is like talking to a person who can only paint his toes because that is all he can see. To a philosopher worst, his life hangs on the word 'perceive', mention the intuitive, the visionary and you mention anathema. It is perhaps that this reality of the unconscious is a new art that is so unmentionable to those who haven't taken it into their calculations, moreso perhaps it is a forgotten art that is again demanding at the mind of humankind, this time a modern mind. That there is no limit to the unconscious and therefore its landscape, that it takes intrepid beings who value themselves but are filled with endurance and the recklessness to travel them, that one must discard utterly conventional reality and even the reality of primary instincts to passage them is all self-evident; cynics and speculators are showing their weakness, not their strengths.

It is not the place or even the dimensions of place one deals with it is the quality that is there.

Its intelligence.

… it's these places that hold my addiction, my obsession, beyond anything else they are the way I see the world albeit it is not what the common populace call the world. It is what they call madness and fear.

It is that one thing sparks off another and then another and I am never truly finished. I am encountering the BLOK but whilst it is applying its enormous capacity to crush and terrorise I am in another place just as outlandish and the BLOK is exerting itself upon something that does not exist, soon it will be open to me, open and moist.

It's strange to look at such devastation as has occurred in my life but therein was the first great gift that I asked of madness, a child's wish, that nothing be terminally broken.

I am again in 1989 the pillars of my world are shattering one after another as I make further advances into chaos, as I journey deeper into the chasm. There are times also when I can confine my presence in the bare inner city flat although the chasm never leaves my sight. There is something black about me, a figure about me as I lay in a semi-coma, it is taking care of 'things'. I have paired. My intuition is about the place as a separate entity; what's more it is having meetings with my shadow on the balcony, the neighbours are already calling me a black magician, something important is brewing, I can feel it. Enter Osu, the spirit who walks like a man; at first weak, weary and beleaguered – it is an invalid nursing back to health; an invalid but I feel the inestimable power about him and he feels a resolve in me that cannot be broken. Later he becomes well, then and only then does one gain anything of an impression of his power, he is like all the motors of a battleship contained in a five foot stature. An impenetrable being. The intuition again lives within me and the shadow dies and for what seems like a great period of time I am without one but death is different for him and he is not permanently so although the grief of parting even temporarily between us is agonising.

It is tonight that I have made the first solid contact with the every-spirit for whom there is no difference between sound and feeling, circumstance and emotion, life and death. It is a tentative approach on his behalf, he wants a place to live, a calamity has befallen and I am not at all opposed to this. It is of utmost interest living with spirits of prominent nature, it is even that these are unnoticed by the general populace … the talent to see and be involved with them comes not so much from sensitivity. I have long held the word suspect since it came to be an aphorism for weakness with even those maligning it wanting to be recognised as such. Alas, it seems impossible for the populace to accept the illogical even though their lives are built on the irrational and illogical and they do quite well.

Contact with the realm of spirits is the same, unnoticed and with no place in vision there is no stress and no discarding of a belief because it never needs to be expressed, you have a vapour world then not a spirit realm, there is nothing of density, nothing to see, nothing of which to experience: should the spirit become powerful and within one's view such is to conflict over this treasured morsel 'logical', that a nervous breakdown often ensues. This is termed garden-variety schizophrenia and its onslaught is typified by not being able to put the square pegs in the round holes, likewise the round pegs in the square holes.

What is a spirit though? People seem to have a hatred at there being no graspable definition, nothing they can spread out on the table with their morning coffee and so they don't exist, they are not put into the too hard basket because they may propagate and then the thing will be full of spooks and unusable.

11.7.93
Sydney

I have been getting messages from Gunther: 'pay up or else!!!' When I purchased Gunther Deix's oil painting I knew it would involve a virtual fight to the death and now that there is only a paltry twelve dollars left to pay he is fuming under the collar; if he could afford the train fare he would probably come from Mittagong on the express and demand satisfaction. You should have seen the aplomb with which he accepted the hundred dollar bills I gave him, 'O, what's this? Money?' He represents an unusual case, he is the Rational man but each square is taken up by a substantial helping of something, here a bit of lunacy, there a bit of the demented, here a bit of the obsessive, there a bit of the absolutely incoherent, here a bit of the genius, there a bit of the chef who is only employed because he burns the soup and must be further employed to cook more soup – which he burns. Nevertheless, it is good to see a truly brazen affair made out of art, it makes it clean, too many times I have come away after the mandatory shaking of hands with something called 'a contemporary artist' to find that my hand stinks.

Deix makes his art from his intensity, which is why there is so much difficulty about him and much of it pursues the concerns of outsider art, women occur greatly in his art but the constant and final is an obsession in every detail with the spirit world which the spirit world seems not only to tolerate but to promote then it is put in readable form with the great things of human complexity as a frame. The man paints death with choice little lipstick hearts.

Perhaps it is that I have lived such a catastrophe-ridden life that I am so interested in resurrection. The unconscious is impersonal about the damage that is done to one and can penetrate to everything, it is one of the sides of its violence, for those that travel there calamities are unavoidable. The longer one remains there the less chance one retains of being a human being. With these wounded and dead things of self there is journey in itself as a remedy. Moreso there is the unlocking of the secrets of their deaths and for their 'resurrection' which is where my talent for intrigue lies. One journey that produces a Horror in the Soul begets another that produces a Coney Island of the Mind. Somewhere in that derelict fun fair you have come upon in that Isthmus of the Unconscious is an empty ice cream cone with a message in it explaining all and giving the unknown location of that missing part of yourself, like a fortune cookie it may be the bestowing of total providence, laws of reality are alterable here and death may be tricked as easily as swindled. What is more, this dwelling with risk and fissure to oneself is prolific, it is like a game of jacks where the adept and adroit may acquire the precious internal life forms that make real life possible at an astounding rate – it is not in the game to lose anything to the hiatus of the unconscious nor the objet it may bring into your path.

PARADOX

Lava flows of supercooled ice through catacombs, volcanic eruptions of molten dust through the labyrinth these things embedded in the eye of some creature, some deity I have discovered for I always thought the core of the animalistic would be a place not a beast and to find these things embedded in its eyes leads to a surprise that leaves the beast forgotten … what-is-more it is not as one would suspect for instead of the wild erotic and curvaceous forms and strange heats one is led to expect one experiences a slow single-minded goring and an approaching blackness that gets larger and larger as one sees more and more of the secrets of life.

It is with great trepidation that one views this place … I might say that the constant goring, the endless pictures that show the seams of so much of what we call life seem somehow the answers and at the same time a robbery. It seems to have been a mistake to leave the black chess board realm of the psychotic where each little square is glued to the other by a cliff and a chasm and where the quaint and funny houses black and white each one occupying one square with opposite and opposite end yet again opposite and where the little black and white houses laugh and pull funny expressions and then frown and then crack ridiculous jokes.

UNEARTHING THE TERMITE LION

So strange to carry something dead about within you. It is sometimes to no avail how many efforts and how many magics one makes, things just come alive again independently, as they will. I cannot even find the reason for death for this creature such was the turmoil surrounding his departure and it seems he was shattered in so many pieces, so that there was nothing to make a completeness again, so many of the pieces were in unknown places, and anyway they were just pieces of a body.

The totem is a lucky one though, although within constraints it is similar to the Egyptian scarab and is not wholly terminated by death – it can passage the Netherworld should it be snuffed. Really all my efforts in this case accounted for nil yet I can see the thing coming alive before my eyes – therein is all of the magician's art.

Chaos has a power, that it can make mobile and elasticise any weight; no dimension or property is changed yet the weight loses all effort and nothing of the mind needs to concern it. It is that it is forgotten right within your constant attention.

The closest I can think to this is that ecstasy of lovers that defies the gravity of things by seeing the ridiculousness of laws.

1.8.93
Sydney

I can barely communicate anymore and it's not for lack of the English language; rather, it's that so many words have been included in their entirety, every exploration, conquest, defeat, has an aftermath which must be survived as well, it is that one's vocabulary becomes realer and realer – onslaught, seething, impaired, broken, impaled, devastated, deforested, splintered, reduced, disassociated, made into pieces, asphyxiant, made finite, made apart, made separate, asundered, damaged, split, fractured, cracked, divided, made a portion, starved, inflamed, broken into, sacked, immolated ... Yet this is only conceivable in a duality and there is its option, entranced, enraptured, enthralled, captivated, titillated, explained, made more, widened, deepened, enriched, given divinity, given power, made resolute, becoming unconquerable, a land in oneself. ... the termite lion came back one night with a woman in his jaws, she was meant for me.

It is interesting this place the BLOK. It has cut me off from everything. It has put a famine upon me to try to stop me plundering it. I have already used up all my body fat and now I am burning up muscle to continue, sinew. But I have an endurance much greater than it estimates and it is a trained and veteran endurance. It is underestimating me and the more it does so the closer I am to having it.

Still I walked in like a fool and its first play was to cut the source of every energy from me. My body screams, there is a continual attempt to smash the centre, there no longer seems to be a way of retreat, but I do not really wish one ...

I see women wrapped in giant leaves like the tobacco inside cigarettes.

22.8.93
Sydney

I see enormous verdant growing from the cunts of women that gives an import to the word lush that my body has never known I see the dead illusions of my life in a jocular man who approaches me with his hand outstretched saying 'lest we forget', I see the blood wash from my hands and the police car take the wrong street turn-off as I leave his body complete with a cut throat, my study of psychopathy was far too long and intense but it was useful, I see the outlandish plant life of this place, I feel I am practising occult buggery with Hieronymus Bosch in one of his sickest and most drugged gardens, compacting bit by bit into a coal with a bite like grasping a handful of broken razor blades, I see all the sensuality I have ever wished coming down the street in a dress that will hardly allow her to walk and black stockings to the boots and am too tied up by the Gulliverian little strings to take her aside and order our clothes off, I see the drugged lunatic in a hell which only seems a second-hand living room to those not in it, begging for understanding, I kick him away, I am only free from the same hell because there is nothing to understand, I see the weariness of the thing I want to find here being the last thing I will find here, I see a fountain of women their vaginas made knotted by streams of plush water and below bathing the first violence of their breasts in it, I see people dissected, things, ideas, visions, ideals, ambitions, reasons for being the same, the parts a mess, inaudible, irretrievable, I see in the black horrible mirror in this place the human race jumping ahead, proliferating only to have it devastate its own creature and sensibility alike as a man with a pocketful of gold will pick on murderous robbers to protect it, but this is only the mirror in this place and I won't look again for more to know.

I see nothing put into nothing, and this is the mystery of the place, I have come upon it early, with this key I will unravel it and assume its power. I see my esoteric hierarchy of knowledge re-established in a few pregnant syringe-ended seconds and the morphine-like indifference I obtained from watching it slowly being destroyed, integer by integer over a decade, nothing changes. I will never cease to believe in the illusion and I save an unavoidable blade and a psychopath's lode for those that damage them. I see a place, why should it be any more than the previous place or the place before that or before that, and so on and so forth.

I see myself so many times fallen by these places that I have learned to actively take notes and examine carefully points of interest whilst emitting the scream that is necessary to emit when you fall and somehow to reassemble part to part in that vacuum that always exists afterwards – it is the most interesting of states, if you are not still capable of the illusion the iron jaws that are clamped about you tear you to flesh.

I see places without reason, things that shouldn't be. I see my myself as a fatted corporation head managing a company of places so numerous that most are forgotten and falling asleep while giving the morning talk to one hundred vice-presidents, cigar ash slowly filling up the half-full whisky glass balanced on my stomach. I see myself with a quick chuckle slowly unlocking the cartouche of yet still another place. I see the place encroaching on me, making ground through my sight as it already has, it will have me see what it wishes eventually and I will be at its behest – from now on sight is not to be trusted, we will proceed the campaign on a deeper level.

If it is of interest, I would like to inform you reader, both with this monstrosity I find myself within and this book. Both are becoming richer, less subsequent to control, more fecund, mistakes are more prevalent, but there is better ground to stand on, I am starting to thirst less, it is like someone has given me a cup of blood to slake my thirst. This place has awoken me, I see things growing everywhere, I see spring; even though it is; I am no good as a domestic general, I need campaigns, their clamour and confusion, left without I become blunt, soggy. I cannot live without risk. My seeings before could have gone on endlessly, there is nothing to segregate them from a youth's lysergic acid adventure or a good bang of the T.H.C. gibberish but one thing happened that through the clamorous static and impaired perception I saw the intelligence of this place and I saw it clearly, where others become imbued with lust or greed to climax their adventure I become impersonal and efficient with the air of an executioner.

The things seem to be returning after my issue from the Core. For months I have been plagued with a severe exhaustion and the chemico-therapy courtesy of Rozelle Psychiatric Hospital did nothing to dispel this, the opposite, in fact. It seems I drew on future reserves, the life force, actually, and then heavily. Those things that make one a cosmology, a world ceased to be, I could not find them. But it seems it has all been a grand game of jacks for high stakes, I have the things I wish albeit some are different from how I saw them at a distance, quite possibly my health will return which somewhat surprises me, I didn't think myself capable, and the old things that it seemed were blown to the four corners of the earth or else mysteriously disappeared are coming tramping back with their fake pomp and mischievous smiles which seem to be saying, we only left when it got dangerous – no wonder it's spring for me.

Of the Core, I know not what to make of it. On the level of contemporary reality I have an unaccountable cold, violent blaze of four months of amnesia, one cannot accept such reality to be factual or content and I am loath to alter my current reality to examine those four months, I will just have to remain the iceberg below the water as the journey was; but don't be misled, I know where it is, and can put my hand below the water to take from it.

It's what I always wanted, my own personal chunk of the Unconscious – I regard it with the same affection one has when one keeps an old tooth filling in the top drawer of the desk.

A SMALL THOUGHT, DECORATION

One of the aspects of power is its seemingly unending intricacies, this one might call its violence. Art brut makers are cunning users of power.

One can no less expect this art to manifest than through the quest for mastery of power. With this 'ascent' there also comes the obedience to the fragilities and vulnerabilities of the endless expression of devices, illusions, decorations, repetitions, animations, systems, and dreams.

The art of decoration is so ever present and widespread in this art brut as a device that one suspects a fundamental preface; for a while the building seems nothing but facade.

It is the basic source of building blocks from which art brut makers devise their individual cosmologies.

It is that the idea and the feeling are the same thing which make this decoration a force rather than a digression.

A HORRIBLE SONNET
for Tony Mannix

Horror is a commodity, a product, an edible product, is
therefore nutritious.

Yes, we have no bananas, but we do have horror.
On the gargantuan body of Horror – each bite in its proper
place.
Spiced with Horror – another pound of flesh.
From my window I threw out a lord's supper – Horror.
And who should find it? – to Horror, a plump pretender.
Who, stuffed to the gills, would undo it, Horror, with pre-
posterous, an abra-
cadabra,.
Is currently at 64% – Horror, but on the rise, obviously.
Is closely associated with a recent excavation – Horror – Cro-
Magnon, piles of teeth, testicles,
vaginas.
Woe unto you if you've kept the shape that Mother (Horror) gave.
Summoned forth (from a warm bed) by peels of it – Horror.
Alas, a lapse (laudable?) from a high horse – Horror.
Out of daylights are we done by it – Horror.
"Horror is my honeybunch."

Phillip Hammial – Sydney
(behind Wynyard Station
April 22, 1986)

WHAT IS THE MATTER WITH LUNATICS?

It seems they are in possession of some fundamental power yet the jibberish and static that they constantly atone to seems to eat into this power like acid, the beauty of the illusion they have managed to grasp is turned into a horror of brokenness by violence and unpredictability. It is unsettling to realize that the smelly, unkempt bum that has just cadged money from you on the street is both extraordinary and dangerous; to himself, to you and to society.

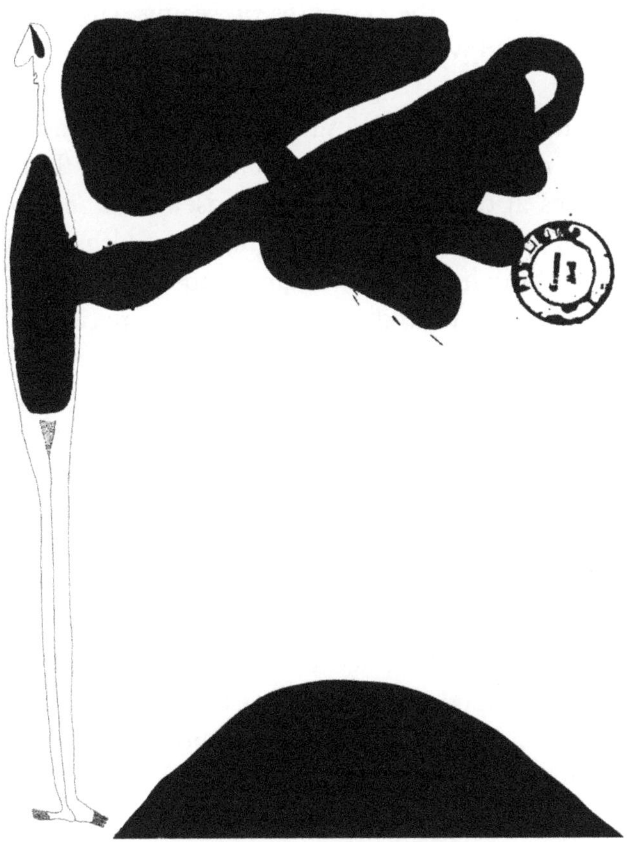

The word which is so favoured, schizophrenia, is such a misnomer that it is irrelevant. Literally, it depicts a broken core, but society is rife with those that remain pedestrian and unnoticed. Of those that are given the name, what they are undergoing is much more proliferate.

What of the madman using the creative powers of the unconscious, yin, anima, persona, ego, to reassemble or reiterate the core? Is he broken, even if such a process is being undertaken with a violence and lack of the logical as to have him defined as schizophrenic? Coherency is ultimately a deeper thing than the simple test a psychiatrist puts one to for the purposes of seeing whether they required a hospital, and will remain so.

Nevertheless, the lunatic is rife. All sorts of unusual things are occurring; there's no way to put them to any test. The lunatic is in a score of places at once, travelling a landscape of violence, performing burials and resurrections, births and deaths; it is with a singular quality though that a madman stands apart, is an outsider and usually creates an unpredictable terror, for a period of time at least, controls his or her own destiny and absolutely so. When the hounds and straitjackets are called for the first thing the screws in hospital operate on is this. It is not allowed. You are lucky if you are allowed partial imagination and some memory.

It's the breakfast room of Rozelle Psychiatric Hospital, Ward 24. Every morning for the past three weeks there has been an eruption of violence. It has been with a great amount of cunning that I have avoided this. Either timed to be outside or huddled in the far corner I have avoided the knives, smashed crockery and thrown breakfasts. This morning is my undoing though, I have become excessive. Wanting the safest place to be I have chosen to sit next to the cripple Peter Linford. The breakfast goes peacefully, I am proceeding from my bacon to my eggs when Peter mutters: "What the hell." He then takes a knife from the table and holds it to my throat, "My name is Peter Linford and I want to go home," he says.

There's nothing very much new you can teach a Psychiatric hospital patient about Surrealism. It is like you enter a Surrealist exhibition when you come to one of these places. It is the gap between illusion and reality and most of your time is taken up trying to forget the works after you've seen them. Breton, Picasso, Dali all missed out on a wealth of material by avoiding being interned. The only living writer that gets my dues on the matter is William S Burroughs, but I think he has built some kind of private mental hospital for himself anyway and they, whoever or whatever he engineered to be the screws, wont let him out. Artaud seems alright he just had a language problem and stayed with his sources. I read Peter Kocan on his years of internment in Morriset for wounding Calwell, leader of the labour party. At one point in time they gave him some nasty pills and his mother came and saved him. Half his luck, most sunny days at Rozelle you can judge an hour passing by the number of patients that collapse on the grounds – when ten or more bodies are prone its time to go in for lunch. In fact since clozapine has been introduced in quantity the place has gone deathly quiet; that is except for breakfast, pills are administered fifteen minutes before breakfast, they generally need half an hour before becoming effective.

Although first-hand knowledge has taken me through a dozen drugs including what was documented in the 1983 Richmond Report as a prolonged near-fatal course of Fluphenazine. I still don't know what gives with the stuff. Every different pill is a new surprise. Hospital inmates rush when the word 'side-effects' is mentioned and the atmosphere of anguish stands with the most desolate chords of French existentialism.

It's early summer, there is that flower heat, bees, dust, honey, nostalgias of freedoms found in school holidays, Peter Linford comes up to me, I can see no tears in his face, it's not that sort of matter, I know he's going to confide in me but here you can't deny that either; as well as no hiding place there's no own-space, it's impossible to go anywhere.

Today is the fifteenth day in succession he has unsuccessfully tried to masturbate. He is on Modecate. His dick is raw he says. It's in there somewhere he says. It's a small enough right to ask. Even most impotent men in sex can manage to masturbate. Libby told me the same thing, you feel nothing. She still has herself screwed at least once a day in a closeted part of the hospital grounds though, "just to feel it go in".

The nurses are all doing well though; big tits, hot blood, flaring rumps, it's no wonder none of them want to go near the medicine room, it might rub off; the male psychiatric nurses all arrive at six in the morning with that fine polo-neck plush look of having gotten your end in the night before.

I am on the same drug as Peter Linford but I have more success, I have a better system. I pick the most obnoxious female cunt the ward possesses and go at it till I deliver the load.

Afterwards, I descend from the bedroom and draw erotic pictures of my next victim. I rationalize that my psychopath leanings will diminish along with the drug and so I am oblivious with my portion of the joy of sex.

I no longer masturbate on the grounds since the gardener who is disturbed tried to run me over with a motor-mower.

Erotic drawing is hazardous for a reason I have yet to understand fully.

Perhaps that it speeds up the metabolism to a breakneck pace, perhaps that it brings to the forefront those esoteric and occult matters of a pluralistic existence that you are always at the precipice; perhaps one deals with a power, like the mind, virtually untouched, yet it is different. It is completely unclad.

The erotic has its union with the unconscious. In what is conscious there are at least two distractions for every impelling thing.

2.9.93
Sydney

It's difficult to know what to do. I was born a shaman, somehow already initiated into the occult. LSD causes no effect of any significance save the release of serotonin into the bloodstream in excess. I was born with a serotonin excess. I feel I'm before my time. Look as I want in the unemployed advertisements, nowhere does it say 'explorer of the unconscious wanted'. Adept at everything I am good for nothing. This place the unconscious demands everything, I cannot even choose a woman unless it approves. In future years they will wonder about this person who glutted himself on it whilst most people choose a drug of some form or dimension to keep it at bay. It is on the increase the unconscious, whether this is liked or not. I can contend it to no parallel except space. I have long realized that there is no coming to the bottom of it, I don't care what fancy coffee table edition you show me. Indisputably I went mad once because it became apparent to me that this place is infinite. I became sane again when I could register that this place is accessible to infinite invention. They will wonder in the future also what barbarism they have put revelation to. But this is nothing new, William Blake's vehemence about the same thing is almost three hundred years old. But this is an evolutionary change, this unconscious. If you look you will see that you yourselves have demanded it. You wanted a new frontier that was egalitarian. Best of luck.

There is one problem though, opening yourselves to the unconscious is to open yourself to everything. I think of Henry Miller. One prophetic statement that is hidden in his writing like a grenade and that is to grow we must experience a growth in the human heart. You have no choice with the unconscious, it consumes the measly. The massive plethora of unconscious reality is offering you itself, not trying to devour you. The sooner we come to live our five thousand year mythology the better. This place is irrepressible and doesn't care about time or process regardless of how many reformations, industrial revolutions or depressions you throw in its way.

It will always grow.

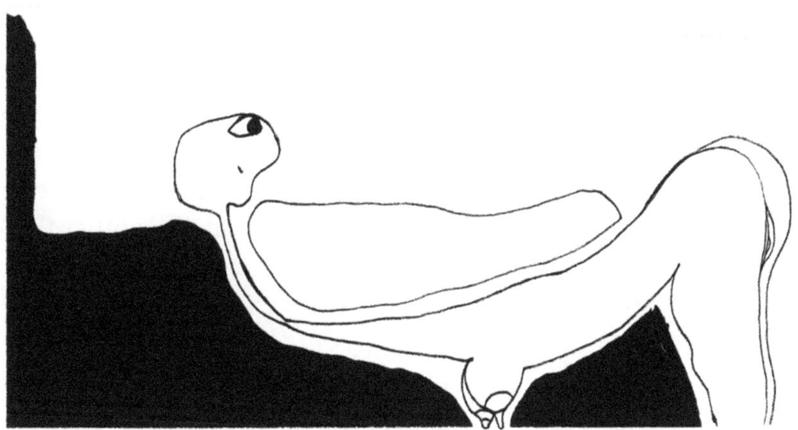

I can't make heads or tails of Peter Linford. His mother delivered him to the admissions ward in the dead of night as if he were the family secret to be hidden away. I think she was weeping because she wasn't compassionless and couldn't have him disposed of at one of the hospital cottages. Peter Linford didn't realize that he was in the unconscious, he still thought he was at school before he got that bump on his head which turned him into a cripple, he couldn't understand why he was seeing things, it was the devil. My fondest memories of him were refusing to budge. He was collapsed on the stairs with two thugs in the employ of the health dept. one on each arm trying to drag him up the first floor stairs (a cripple yet!) with the thug that was a retired New Zealand N.C.O. bad-mouthing him. Nothing could be done, Peter Linford had had enough, he became heavier-than-lead.

THE UNCONSCIOUS

As I have said earlier I can make almost no sense of 4 months spent in the core of psychosis; there is no time sequence for this four months although I can map it off roughly on a calendar, but it won't apply to seconds, minutes, hours, days, or weeks. Indisputably it is the core, nothing else could knock one so senseless. Learning that there is an infinity of the Unconscious was a big thing, it showed me I could be a big fish in a big pond. The other thing was a poetry to life so beautiful as to be intoxicating and heartbreaking at the same time. As yet I cannot even touch the door that has been opened, but I can see some of what is within. The other thing remains although it disperses and that is a trauma and shock to the brain which lessened my capacity to be myself.

It is hard to express the pertaining power of reality. It only exists where there is a perspective and such we no longer have, we have gone past it. All encompassing in the renaissance, Grosz was merrily putting nails in its coffin in the 30's. It means a war is as important as the vein that will take you to something in yourself. It means that there is no scale to hardship no relativity between the micro and macro systems and better off we are for it. It was artificial, true reality is indivisible.

It is reality that is being talked about in this book, reality is what most books talk about. It is one thing though to be able to perceive a reality and another to alter it. There is a double and second meaning which is not noticed when I refer to altered states. The average sane person can effect reality and be affected in turn by it, the lunatic is incongruous and alters it.

With every lunatic there is something of the shaman, something of the magician, often a great deal of the psychic although the processes of social control and what hides behind them have often planted them six foot under.

More than a decade and a half ago when I was doing a brief stint at a university I came across an anthropology book which I bought for the cover and title; it was titled "The Hero with a Thousand Faces" and I still feel that with a title like that it should have talked about the madman.

Two nights ago a programme on outsider artists ran on national television. Who should I see but George Karnikowski. You take your life in your hands when you go and see George, you may be fed Danish cheese, you may be fed cornflakes on cold spaghetti, on one occasion when I went to his house after art he sold me a pair of pants. There he was on television being pampered, absolutely in his element.

One foot was at least Matisse, the other Cezanne and they had the privilege to transport the head of G. Karnikowski about while he made pictures. All is as it should be. George said if one could see the fifty or sixty pictures he has made in a room "lumped together" one would be different. I know what he is talking about, these are fifty or sixty of his heads and they have gone elsewhere, into other hands and he cannot say at any time "look" but that is a sadness sometimes common to artists. When he is saying you would be different in this room he is saying you would see the Hero and be different.

Anthony Hopkins was a delight after talking and showing space orbs and wizard lights. He talks simply I think because the worlds he is involved with will not parley with any doubletalk. It was only during this television programme that I became aware of him as such a psychically powerful and complex individual although I have long been aware of his development being his own and of his art being a small instrument he played sublimely.

To my great joy who should the programme conclude with but Phillip Heckenberg. When I say it was a joy I am not kidding, when I first met him in 1987 he was going down for the fifth time and was still magically somehow still afloat. There he was with an adroitness and power that makes the things he is making contest with, say, Joseph Beuys. He has command of things now, he never had to alter himself, just alter his altered environment. The thousand heads are all one for him, all have right to speak or not depending upon how they feel.

the BLOK

It is this place, the BLOK, which is worrying me. It is winning. It has a slow eroding power which gains a little ground every day. All I have is this new thing, my will. Everything else met massive impact in the Core. I cannot summon up either an agility or a violence yet. I will be thrown into its pit, into its stomach if I do. I often think of the happy times between wars. Exhaustion and resilience do not co-habit. It is turning into a war of attrition. This for one more head.

I have noticed an unusual situation, that I have lost my head, that it has been removed for some reason. It is good I have noticed this because the strange feeling of not having a head was driving me to distraction. But then, I have been without a head before, that was in the early part of the 1980s. It is the shadow that does this, my art tells me so, but the way it is gone no words can be put to, save that for all its profundity it is rather ridiculous like watching the tail of a small lizard wriggle about after becoming disconnected. I am not overly concerned, I am not going off to my local general practitioner over the matter, anyway the shadow gives great gifts and should always be respected for that, it is just that they are not encountered in the normal day to day affair of gift-giving and are too porous to hold any logic. I cannot say I am distressed not having a head, it is a certain liberty and presumably I will grow another as before.

I am disagreeable at the moment. It is that I have come to the top of the heap in this matter of madness and like a reptile shedding its skin will bite anything trying to disturb my reverie of passage. I am no longer an alien looking out through some subterranean watery sight upon your workings and doing, I am one of you now and you'll just have to put up with that. Or almost. But I don't consider your lives utterly wasted, just frantic, as if your bodies are too heavy for the fine logic out of which you build the chassis for your vehicles: you are always having accidents and standing in the middle of the street for hours having debates over them. Sometimes they are blood-curdling like the Council yard I visited at night packed with vehicles from fatalities. There were ghosts everywhere, some still pushing their foot down on the accelerator. Never have I been in a place with such an atmosphere of end, nothing could be done about these things, this was total captivity.

The concrete world proliferates in what is a combination of the absurd and damning, the insane world is different with these things, there is no insurance cover for damnation here, not even third party, no insurance company will touch you, yet when you come upon the absurd which may be never-ending it is an entertainment of vitality and freedom and not the censure of something indecipherable or something gone wrong.

I am in a place, the old is dissolving, it's that I have carefully and fastidiously selected the treasures and implements of twenty years of campaign and warfare from amongst a plethora and a chasm is rapidly opening between me and the past. It is that others are giving me their greetings and saying that they know this experience, but they do not. I can see to the very bottom of this chasm.
I am well aware I am not in step with those changes that are the

subterranean happenings of our milieu, I don't mean the fashions or the fads I am observant of that, I refer to the sub-structural alteration, the incongruities, fissures and dissonances stemming from the collective unconscious to the matter. I'm not intelligent, sentient, I do not operate from thoughts and the brain but from awareness and the body. It gives me the predatory nature of a wolf from a barren place where nothing is taken for granted. I have been in the unconscious so long that this collective unconscious is often very transparent.

I came to understand the force of sanity and the polemics of difficulty with which it is employed in society from a psychopath. I came to recognize it in people when I saw it, and I usually didn't have to look it was on display and I came to realize that here we had the freaks of society, congenital birth deformities the lot, with shaven heads and saddleback noses courtesy of their syphilitic mother: Sanity.

Strange also how the parasites are coming about those explorers of the Unconscious. The BLOK. Here in this place everything is riches and everything is impossible – a bloody truncated dog's head is its totem. It is a place of sores – even the landscape has sores, and where the most outlandish thoughts mix with the most mundane and are indistinguishable from each other.

I use a variety of weapons, tools and implements to savage, journey, enamour and plunder my way through states of being that don't solely reside within me, but are more.

There is one alone though that is constant and unerring because it will always integrate the elements of chaos, with this I have never let a point become affixed I can determine where it is and what I am, anywhere. This making of art.

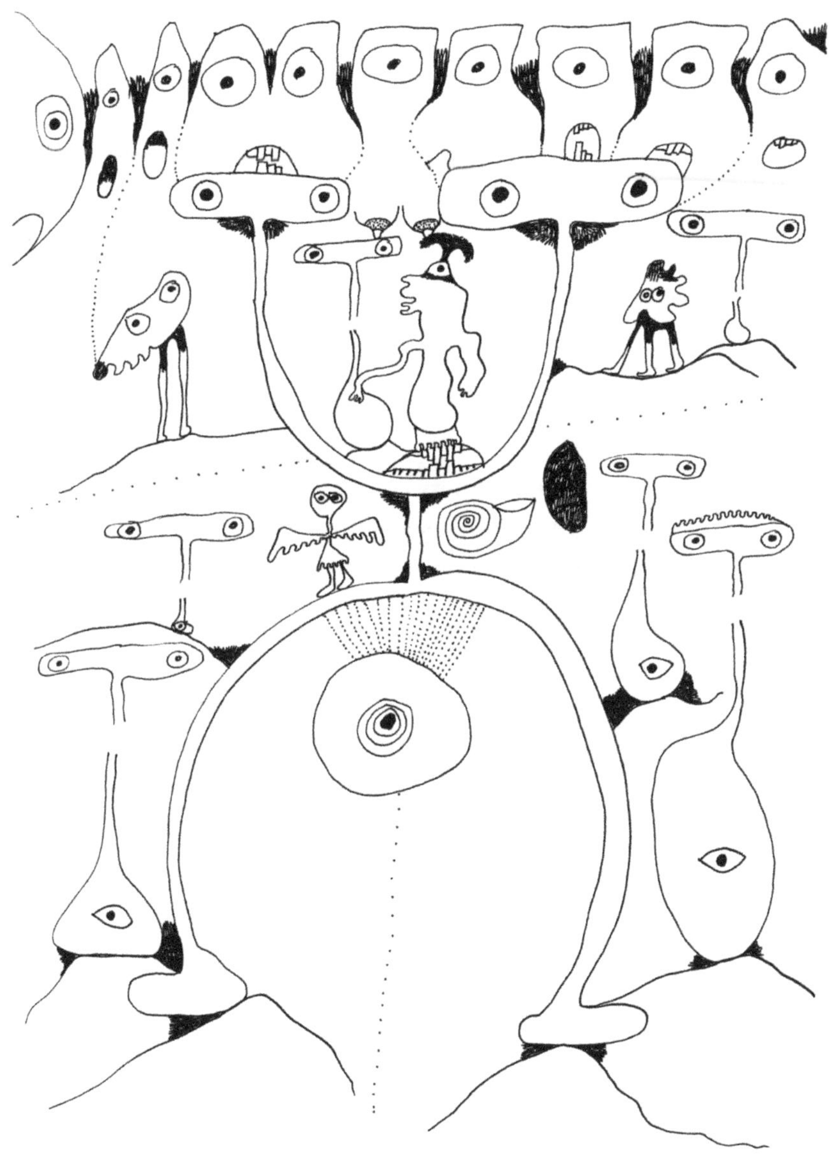

This making of art has been about constantly for over a decade, but now a new idea has been literally striking me …

that I am on the threshold of creating

a being-of-art

rather than a body-of-work.

It is often now that I am hunting about inside of myself
to find that tiny vein which must be added
to the body
to make it a being.

It is the absolute wildness of such a thing
which I find vast that has freed my pen again,
and its trueness that has keep it consistent.

I see black spaces in the night now

the engrossing order of our human progression

went around their wildness

it didn't subjugate them.

They are the progressive things,
they still have teeth

they can still taste warm blood.

In this role as Frankenstein with my world of art I see nothing but success, sometimes I think its all been happening in reverse, that it is its intelligence recreating, retrieving me from a violent and horrible death past.

I listen to the rocks move in the black spaces,
the rocks are masoned,
        like pyramid masonry yet they come at all angles
        and all valley;
        the din is like a solid waterfall

        that comes from the hole that was put by a bullet
        between the eyes of the moon …

I hear an old woman fall through the floor
I hear
the she-wolf scream
        I hear the clown shriek
        I hear the sadist whine,
        I hear the animal hold itself
                in its own jaws;
                eventually I can hear nothing more

                except the din

        for which there is no metaphor …

The People's Odyssey

On Philip Heckenberg

The lazy green drives through the acrid black force on wheels of yellow fire. See the things there are to see this morning. The unconscious is like a slither of razor. Like a small brittle piece of moon, humming with amber honey but infinitely sharp. It can cut the flesh from the bone. The tumour from the brain. The thought from the moment. Fire into flesh. Flesh into ash. Ash into brain cells. Brain cells into steel. Steel into ether. Ether into machine. A machine which drives you on wheels of sinew. Slowly inevitably towards a chasm which consumes everything.

All this from a little slither of moon. Such profundity. It makes my face lopsided though as if I am an idiot or know too much about psychopathological things. Do you see how in this vision everything is misfit? The wheels steer the car. The axle is the radio aerial. The body melts like an ice cream in the sun. The exhaust goes up a passenger's ass. No wonder it's heading towards the brink. With technology like this we will create a world that is truly life-like.

The hyper-erotic demons, one with a voluptuous woman's body. The other male who's erect and being groped by her. Drops of semen flow to the ground. Impossible heads gleam at each other with dissonant intense eyes focused, horns and fangs protrude. It's quite impossible to tell who is getting the better of whom. Large clawed feet dance on a wobbly ballroom floor, although startlingly close the couple will ring with decorous babies. Everything is muscle, tissue, sex organs. Nothing is quiet, unmoving. Because of the distortion it's an exercise in debauchery. Dihatha sava morning erecto-misanthrope.

The magic chant goes on forever. See the small movement of the genitalia. See how it's amplified into a thunderous crescendo. Every sound is here, from the railway train to the raindrop. From the siren to the bird song. From the impasse to the achievement. Nevertheless the crude black and white pit remains gathering focus, gathering that identity-less compaction in every drawing. See how the black mass of a dark mind rains. Nowhere is there any space even to exist, yet they seethe with thickening cognition. You cannot keep identity here, nor content. Only the basic matter of life.

All the black places of life are assembled for you to peruse, but this is not the word. Dwell likewise in an eerie and alarming rendition. You get the impression after a little that the artist is not painting in black ink, but in his own blood. We are dealing with a ritual, not a process. See how small you are in this vision. You are the smallest dot in a scenario of Titanic black proportions. In the clamour of a war that has existed for millions of years of evolution. What is in the mind? To what point is its own ruthless entity? Demolishing sentiment to make the essential heavy metal fact.

On Janine Hilder

One. A glance. Shrill eyes of flesh pouring from their sockets, a steely squint-eyed train streaks through the brain passage, which dumps its freight of hot molten damsels in a damp blue place and rattles onwards. In worlds where sympathy doesn't matter. The metal and feeler-like quality of awareness again screams, and the pounding of the vermillion blood in the vermillion ears hearing vermillion screams. At what hour does hope die, roped to the train track inside a fanatical black brain? Every hour, every minute, every second, yet the infant remains at the core, although composed of plastic features one can never grasp.

One way of seeing things is from the bottom up, the core, the raison d'être. A piece becomes the whole. Likewise, the whole breaks down into pieces. At what point does one call a halt to it, or is it the never ending push to succeed with self? What species of belief, what species of being? There is more mystery than substance allows. You almost expect to experience a practical joke behind some of the images, and they are so quaint like girl guides or bums that have lost their way or cats without tails. In this intricate confusion, everything has a purpose, and love's knot is always being tied.

Two. A frenzy of line is entangled with pathos and anticipation in the pit of the stomach, and mimics a sort of creation pregnancy. Out of a hairline crack in the abdomen, crawling up the thorax, all sorts of infra-sensitive creatures of the persona. A birth is like an infestation. The clock is perpetually at one minute to 12:00 PM. The witching hour.

Strange hominid shapes fly through the night sky. It is full moon also. Everything hums with passion, lightness, poignancy, the sentimental, affairs of the person in romance, the sinister, the quizzical, the unintelligible, the haphazard configuration that is life. A psychic mystery far too great to comprehend presents itself. All we can hope to do is to examine the individual pieces of the puzzle for clues, gestures, nuances, and the speculation which might take us further and deeper into a place with endless signposts but no recognizable features.

On George Karnikowski

A brooding vase of flowers assures you life is worth living. And there are no strings attached, but the romantic is black, or rather a bit eccentric. A bit strange. As if these pictures are being created by a watch maker, complete with eye glasses, protruding tummy and old paint. George is each of his picture's beloved uncle and its confessor. It is intimate with him no matter what it is, no matter where it goes. Vase after vase of electric flowers line the gallery walls and George is the first to take you by the arm and offer you a cigarette and to tell you he's the best artist in the gallery. Perhaps in the world at present. Nothing escapes his eye.

As Aldous Huxley put it, he can ascertain the very Is-ness of something living immediately. Albeit the sum total impression is of a psychotic Santa Claus with his psychotic vision. The absence of death, despair, depression, violence, perseverance. It's almost a girl's dream. Or a beachcomber's. Floating blazing suns on a cross-hatched decorated multi-coloured background. Sound into movement. Movement into colour. Colour into fixation. Fixation into hysterical laughter. Hysterical laughter into caresses.

Forever the world is held at sunrise, and the first birds are chirping more and more brightly. Colourful things are magically appearing with each passing second. Multi-coloured stained glass faces peer over every suburban hedge. It would be just plain psychedelic if it were not so sincere. Narcoleptic birds in a state of placid shock stare at a muddy sun on an ochre horizon. The scene looks doped as if the birds have been injected with still-life beatitude. A cobalt blue woman with black hair sprouts antennae and caresses a radiant pink found object which one can easily imagine is a throbbing heart which is both pulsating and standing still like a hummingbird.

A vine grows out of standing figures and proceeds on a startlingly yellow background. Grows up the spine from the sacrum into the crocodile brain at the rear of the cranium and erupts into China red flowers. The fabulous city of turrets and minarets equalled by no other floats in a sky of vermilion. Pleasant, dopey clouds hang everywhere. The towers are all blazing pink and narcotic and resemble a flock of rampant exquisite peni. Underground a stained glass green world seems to insinuate a hitherto unknown depth to things. A beautiful girl's leg seems bloody and far too intimate. It is a single leg no more. A blood red bird perches on the knee cap. At the top of the leg a fabulous face appears with one yellow eye. Hairs pour down the page. The face tells us a great deal. It is a duck that has misplaced it's bill.

The order of life to George is something to be celebrated, not least of all for the gem it has given him. A place in it, and a dream to have while being in it.

On Anthony Hopkins

A curiously dreamlike army of lighted psychic apparitions, from another earth, play and revel in the mania of Utopia. Nothing about chaos theory here, rather, the ordered and somewhat makeshift dance of the intimate festival of the self. Psychic lights, wizard lights and space orbs dance, carouse, caress, mate in a translucent subconscious that is gossamer soft and malleable, like putty, and yet vegetable crisp.

What becomes slightly alarming, after they have wooed you, is that they are intelligent and sentient lights, with characters like Snow White's dwarves. These are the lights that illuminate the dark recess at the back of the brain during dream, and Tony Hopkins is sitting there, notebook on his lap, casually drawing them. It's a simple world of endlessly varied amoeba without tragedies.

Only the lofty inspiration soul, although somewhere a plaintive sadness echoes endlessly. Not because the lights aren't real, but because only their author sees them. Come to think of it, is it an alien planet he is in communication with, and when will we get to talk to them? I suppose it is the belief in them that makes it, and love, and friendship. So much more than something as hard as them being refracted light from dust particles.

They are Anthony's friends, and we are being introduced to them and their fairy floss warmth, one after the other. Not for the purpose of curiosity, but to learn of good nature and mystery. It is engrossing to think that so many variations can be produced, and none of them have any bad temper.

When everything seemed so well-adjusted, who would suspect a fly in the ointment? But there is. A big one. More like a woolly mammoth in the ointment, really. They are Anthony's black drawings, in which he rails against the concrete structure that has grown about him.

Often accompanied by writing, he attempts to demolish what he sees as negative, and in no tactful manner. He cajoles it to be better, to improve itself, and casts black curses against it when it won't. For it is of a different order, this reality, to the populace of ordered humble beings that he creates, so the black drawings and writings continue, deemed necessary, although they are ineffectual.

Obviously there is no place for such blackness of soul, with its space orbs, wizard lights and other such beings. Anyway, they wouldn't understand it, so the spleen and bile of life finds an explosive offering elsewhere. Somewhere indeed harmless to his cosmology, on another planet, ours, where it seems to be most appropriate.

Meanwhile, in this Utopia he makes, not even a tremor is felt, because he has long since become its doting father, and its inhabitants are too precious to intimidate with the terrors of life.

On Anthony Mannix

"So what?" You may ask. "Here he is. More of his scribbles and his irrational writing. It never makes sense. The grammar is atrocious. He must misspell his words on purpose. Just when it seems you have found something you have lost it. Is this the way his mind works? Or is he doing this to you on purpose? Look, look, there he is again. Writing about things he's got no idea of. He doesn't even use the words properly. He's trying to reinvent them. He will just twist them his way. Bad luck about what they mean."

A scratching on a blackboard, plenty of fingernails screaming, "What black warrior? What black world?" The eyes are fixed on what you'll never see. Don't try you won't be able to understand. A dark figure is nearby, on the march, signifying journey and coming demise. But there is an abundance of demise here. The bottomless pit walks out of a dark alleyway, quoting apparitions of the new moon. One must notice all those teeth like great broken lamb bones.

As for the pit, the more you look, the more the pit. A black populated entity that looks as if it's composed from shredded bats. The background is a myriad of light bulbs. The head is five times the size of the body, and intensely labeled with power words. All in all there is a shrill sound coming from between this entity's teeth that makes you simultaneously both love it, and want to stamp on it and put it in trash.

Life has been one step at a time against and ahead of logic, which is not the same as reality. Reality is entirely subjective, it's made. It's a manufactured article according to what we need. The angel has a banshee for a mouth, and girlies living in its wings like lice. When you look after images of the ghosts in your life trouble, but you realize they are after images.

No respite though, this angel seems puzzled, as if taking a wrong turn on the highway in victorious flight like a martian. His hands grow out of his body three times as fast as his legs. They are having a mania, so is he, but it's a mania in the cold tungsten confine of reality, and not for flight's sake.

Yet another angel, implacable logic like a plum, she wears polka dot britches with a fly. The wingspan is small but she can still leave the ground with a whoosh. Big, haunting, kind eyes full of ashes and love. She has no trouble working out which way to fly, she just goes the direction her breasts point. Flesh pounded upwards into earth, red coals ground downwards into ice. Life ground down into mummification. Confusion speared upwards into thought.

The melting flesh, the molten earth, the acerbic breath of nowhere, the hidden warm oedipal layer of nothingness. I feel a dinosaur that needs a fucking. A face with its conical witch's nose pointing to the full moon walks on spongy, wiry legs. Arms out of cranium and chin. I can't help thinking of an intellectual cockroach with letters after its name. A large eye seems to be strutting by on plasticky, springy legs, looking directly at you. If you had any secrets, you do not now.

Then you notice a nose, it's like the Eiffel Tower. A mouth also appears, with which a startled man is being devoured, or perhaps caressed. A small black cloud of tungsten floats meaningfully by.

An explosion of the feminine large killzone massive buttocks, prodigious breasts, thighs like tree trunks, all bound up in the captivity of nylon. The study of a head, an orange scream embedded in a grass green glacier. Pellets of matter whip about like asteroids, clash. A sea of dots make the pictures both electric and narcotic.

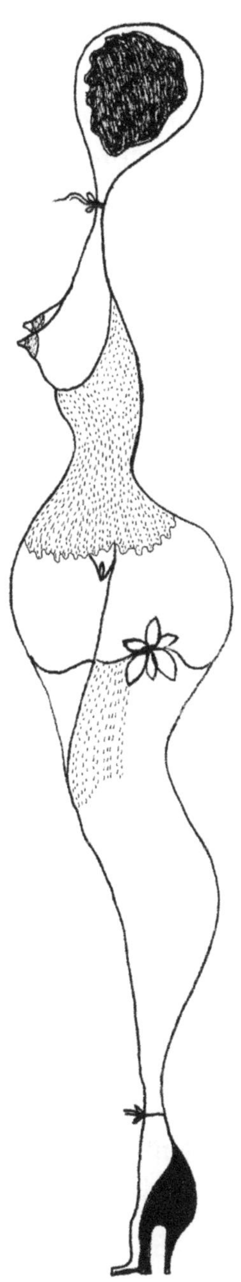

Acknowledgements:

Extracts from "The Skull" and "The Machines or a Concise History of the Machines (as far as I know them ...) ..." have appeared in the following experimental sound recording:

A bead for a small mouth
Anthony Mannix and Graeme Revell, p 1989 Barooni.
https://www.discogs.com/Various-A-Bead-To-A-Small-Mouth/release/100608.

An earlier version of "The Skull" was published as a limited edition hand bound book in collaboration with Carlo Catalano, who contributed images. The book was set up and published by Circa. Publications in 1986.

The Skull quotes from T. S. Eliot's poem "Burnt Norton" and *Meditations* by Marcus Aurelius.

The following works by Philip Hammial appear with his permission in "The Light Bulb Eaters":

"A HORRIBLE SONNET"
"AUTHENTICITY"
"Tony, Upon reflection."

"The People's Odyssey" was recorded by Anthony Mannix and broadcast on ABC Radio National, The Night Air, Outsiders, Sunday 25, January 2004.

I'd like to thank Gareth Jenkins for his invaluable assistance, he healed many of the scars in the manuscript.

I am in communication with this Christ beside me – it's that we have made a pact to do and experience everything illicit that there is. Already my eyes have that absolute comprehension of sin and an incalculable knowingness, observers can see this precisely but they cannot penetrate behind the eyes no matter how hard they try. Already I am seeing strange creatures in strange places and calculating how to get there.

Notes:

1. Artist's Statement: *Handle With Care*, 2008 Adelaide Biennial of Australian Art. Art Gallery of South Australia, Adelaide, 2008. pp38.
2. Atomic Book Digital Archive: https://www.theatomicbook.com/
3. Mo015: Journal of a Madman 1995-96, pp43. All quotes from Mannix's original artist books, are referenced to The Atomic Book archive by Mannix object (Mo) number and page number. To locate the original text search the archive by Mo number. The archive can be accessed via the 'v2008' tab of the website: https://www.theatomicbook.com/
4. Mo012: Journal of a Madman 1994-95, The Atomic Book Archive. pp88.
5. Interview with Mannix by Jenkins, 2018.
6. Mo054: Outsider Writing, The Atomic Book Archive. pp2.
7. Weiss, Allen S. *Phantasmic Radio*, North Carolina, Duke University Press, 1995. pp59.
8. Rasula, Jed and Steve Mc Caffery. *Imagining Language: An Anthology*. Ed.: Cambridge: The MIT Press, 1998.
9. Gérard Genette cites W.D. Whitney's and William James' expression to encapsulate Saussure's position: 'the word dog does not bite', pp360. For Mannix the word dog certainly does have the potential to bite, as the word has the capacity to bring what Mannix experiences as an autonomous dog into being. Thus for Mannix, language, in its various formulations, is a profoundly living entity – intimately connected with his physical and psychic reality. In the realm of lived metaphor, borderlines between signifier and signified collapse, reuniting the written word, thought and referent in such a way that language retains the psychic potential to affect directly the physical body and its surroundings. Language does not represent, it presents. Genette, Gérard. "Valéry and the Poetics of Language." *Textual Strategies: Perspectives in Post-Structuralist Criticism.*

Ed. Josue V. Harari. New York: Cornell University Press, 1979. pp359-73.
10. Square bracket and Ellipsis in original: Mo001: Journal of a Madman No.4, The Atomic Book Archive. pp98.
11. In defining 'defamiliarisation' as a literary term, Shklovsky suggests that 'as perception becomes habitual, it becomes automatic'. In the same way, habitual uses of language deaden its impact, which in turn serves to deaden humanity's experience of the world. Shklovsky's characteristically Modernist aim is to return to original experience, to feel and see as if for the first time, and to present such feelings to an audience in order that their vision is likewise renewed. Shklovsky, V. *Art as Technique. Literary Theory: An Anthology.* Ed. Julie Rivkin. Malden, Mass: Blackwell, 1998. pp17-23.
12. Anthony Mannix. "The Demise." *The Toy of the Spirit.* Ed. Gareth Jenkins. Puncher and Wattmann, 2019. pp89
13. I draw this term from Bill Ashcroft in his book about the poet Francis Webb, *The Gimbols of Unease* (pp70). However, the notion of 'lived metaphor' is a central concept for many authors who have theorised about the schizophrenic experience. Johnston and Holzman in *Assessing Schizophrenic Thinking*, label it 'Concreteness … in which ideas take on an apparent reality' (pp75). Carl Jung suggests that, 'To say that insanity is a dream which has become real is no metaphor' ("Psychogenesis" pp241): Ashcroft, Bill. *The Gimbals of Unease: The Poetry of Francis Webb*. Nedlands: The Centre for Studies in Australian Literature, U of Western Australia, 1996. / Johnston, M. H., P.S. Holzman. *Assessing Schizophrenic Thinking: A Clinical and Research Instrument for Measuring Thought Disorder.* San Francisco: Jossey- Bass, 1979. / Jung, Carl. "On The Psychogenesis of Schizophrenia". *The Psychogenesis of Mental Disease.* Trans.: R.F.C. Hull. London: Routledge & Kegan Paul, 1960. pp233-49.
14. Anthony Mannix. "The Light Bulb Eaters". *The Toy of the Spirit.* Ed. Gareth Jenkins. Puncher and Wattmann, 2019. pp110.
15. Migone, Christof. "Headhole: Malfunctions and Dysfunctions

of an FM Exciter." *TDR: The Drama Review: A Journal of Performance Studies 40.3 (1996)*. pp52.
16. Anthony Mannix. "The Light Bulb Eaters." *The Toy of the Spirit*. Ed. Gareth Jenkins. Puncher and Wattmann, 2019. pp192.
17. Anthony Mannix. "The Demise." *The Toy of the Spirit*. Ed. Gareth Jenkins. Puncher and Wattmann, 2019. pp118.
18. Anthony Mannix. "The Light Bulb Eaters." *The Toy of the Spirit*. Ed. Gareth Jenkins. Puncher and Wattmann, 2018. pp131-132.
19. Mannix's erotic art-making is an attempt to access and express this primary libidinal drive. The process of drawing and writing in Mannix's world-view directly links with this erotic force. Within this practice no activity is more primary than that which he calls 'sex scribble': here form and content become entirely unified in a signifier which brings into dialogue the body's action and passion: 'I first began experimenting with what i call "sex scribble" in my second journal. My early works in sexuality and eroticism were all to précis and not always was i able to express the erotic in a patience, detailed drawing. all too often i would destroy the effect by being forced by the energies i was utilizing to make a 'hasty' drawing. I decide that what was right for the situation was just that and made up 'Sex Scribble' for the times when the expression had to be alacritous.' Mo001: Journal of a Madman No.4, pp 49. For an extended discussion of this see: Jenkins, Gareth S, Anthony Mannix: 'The atomic book', PhD thesis, School of Journalism and Creative Writing, University of Wollongong, 2008. http://ro.uow.edu.au/theses/89. pp135-141.
20. Often erotic in nature, Mannix suggests that any illustration with a wheel on it represents a complete idea. Thus these drawings can be seen as a form of private hieroglyphics – a type of language in which Mannix seeks to express himself while psychotic. For an example see: Mo024: Erogeny: a book of fables about Rozelle Lunatic Asylum. pp2.
21. Here, letters disconnect from any specific denotative meaning, prefacing their sound-value. For an example see: Mo030: Erotoma-

nia No.1. pp5.
22. Mo001: Journal of a Madman No.4, The Atomic Book Archive. pp40.
23. "Anthony Mannix talks to Ulli Beier", *Outsider Art in Australia, Aspect No. 35, 1989*. pp71.
24. Mo012: Journal of a Madman 1994-95, The Atomic Book Archive. pp16.
25. Mo002Journal of a Madman no.5 1988-89, The Atomic Book Archive. pp24.
26. Mo012: Journal of a Madman 1994-95, The Atomic Book Archive. pp174-75.
27. Anthony Mannix. "The Skull." *The Toy of the Spirit*. Ed. Gareth Jenkins. Puncher and Wattmann, 2019. pp73
28.Mo053, Outsider Art Statement, The Atomic Book Archive. pp1.
29. Anthony Mannix. "Dedications" *The Toy of the Spirit*. Ed. Gareth Jenkins. Puncher and Wattmann. 2019. pp46.
30. Ibid pp45.
31. Ibid pp30.
32. This work: *Vehicles Of Refuge, Abundance, Repentance, Jubilation, Beatitude, Transfiguration, Supplication, Etc*: drawings by Anthony Mannix; Poems by Philip Hammial can be found in numerous public collections including Sydney University's Rare Book and Special Collections Library.
33. Mo001: Journal of a Madman No. 4, The Atomic Book Archive. pp81.
34. This recording can be found in 'The Atomic Book Digital Archive': https://www.theatomicbook.com/audio-a-concise-history-of-the-machine. This work appears on the record, A Bead To A Small Mouth, released in 1989 on the Barooni Music label with Graeme Revell. This release also includes Mannix reading from "The Skull" also availabe in the archive where it is called "The Skull (excerpt)", again with Revell. Mannix has done many collaborations with experimental musicians – most commonly with

The Loop Orchestra whose music most approximates, he suggests, the sounds he hears during psychosis.
35. Mo045: The Skull. pp17.
36. Anthony Mannix. “The Skull.” *The Toy of the Spirit*. Ed. Gareth Jenkins. Puncher and Wattmann, 2019. pp71.
37. Ibid pp72.
38. Anthony Mannix. “The Demise.” *The Toy of the Spirit*. Ed. Gareth Jenkins. Puncher and Wattmann, 2019. pp115.
39. Ibid pp91.
40. Ibid pp87.
41. Ibid pp88.
42. Mo046, 'The Light Bulb Eaters', The Atomic Book Archive.
43. Anthony Mannix. “On Anthony Mannix.” *The Toy of the Spirit*. Ed. Gareth Jenkins. Puncher and Wattmann, 2019. pp230.
44. Mo046, ‘The Light Bulb Eaters’, The Atomic Book Archive. pp98.
45. Interview with Mannix by Jenkins, 2017.
46. Cardinal, Roger. Outsider Art. Praeger, 1972. pp10.

Biographical Note:

Anthony Mannix was born in 1953 in Sydney. Studying cultural anthropology at Macquarie University he felt avenue to explore reality and unreality in a continuous book of 'subjective documentation' of text and art. For the last 30 years he has pursued this. He is widely exhibited and published.

Printed in Australia
AUHW011848211019
318878AU00001B/1

9 781925 780284